THE GOSPEL & PERSONAL EVANGELISM

Mark E. Dever

Foreword by C.J. Mahaney

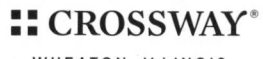

CROSSWAY®

WHEATON, ILLINOIS

The Gospel and Personal Evangelism

Copyright © 2007 by Mark Dever

Published by Crossway
          1300 Crescent Street
          Wheaton, Illinois 60187

Cover art direction: Josh Dennis

Cover design: Luke Daab

Cover illustration: Bridgeman Art Gallery

First printing 2007

Printed in the United States of America

ISBN-13: 978-1-58134-846-0
ISBN-10: 1-58134-846-0
ePub ISBN: 978-1-4335-1879-9
PDF ISBN: 978-1-4335-0204-0
Mobipocket ISBN: 978-1-4335-0339-9

Library of Congress Cataloging-in-Publication Data
Dever, Mark.
  The Gospel and Personal Evangelism / Mark E. Dever;
foreword by C.J. Mahaney.
     p. cm.
  ISBN 978-1-58134-846-0 (tpb)
    1. Evangelistic work. 2. Witness bearing (Christianity) I. Title.
BV3790.D4765   2007
248'.5—dc22   2007016748

Crossway is a publishing ministry of Good News Publishers.

VP		26	25	24	23	22	21	20	19	18	17
23	22	21	20	19	18	17	16	15	14	13	12

With thanks to God
for his faithfulness
in fruit given through evangelism,
now precious friends—John, Karan, Ryan—and in
friends who've taught me about evangelism:

JIM PACKER

WILL METZGER

MACK STILES

and

SEBASTIAN TRAEGER

Contents

Foreword

One of the first things I discovered about my very good friend Mark Dever is that he walks as fast as he talks. It was over ten years ago that I drove from my home church in the suburbs of Washington DC to meet Mark at Capitol Hill Baptist Church, where he serves as senior pastor. It was a pleasant day, so Mark suggested we walk the short distance from his church's historic building to a nearby Subway restaurant. Even though I usually walk at a brisk pace myself, I had trouble keeping up with Mark.

Moments before entering the fast-food establishment, Mark explained that he ate there often, not because of the fine cuisine, but for the purpose of sharing the gospel. Inside, he greeted the owners—a Muslim couple from India—by name and engaged them in friendly conversation.

As we sat down, I began to quiz Mark about his heart for unbelievers and his strategy for sharing the gospel. He told me that he intentionally frequents the same restaurants and businesses so he can develop relationships and hopefully create evangelistic opportunities.

Since that day, I've attempted to follow Mark's example and had the joy of sharing the good news with many people I meet along the seemingly uneventful route of daily life.

If you, like me, have walked through entire days unconcerned and unaware of the lost sinners all around you, or if you desire to share the gospel but are unsure how to build a relationship or start a conversation, *The Gospel and Personal Evangelism* will encourage and equip you. As you read, you will catch Mark's contagious passion to share the gospel of Jesus Christ and receive practical instruction in personal evangelism.

While this book is for all Christians, it is also a gift to pastors. Cultivating evangelism in the local church is one of a pastor's most important responsibilities and difficult challenges. Perhaps *the* most difficult. However, through the pages of *The Gospel and Personal Evangelism,* Mark's wisdom, teaching, and experience will support you in this vital work of ministry.

That's why, for many years now, I've been pestering Mark to write this book. It's so that by the grace of God, church members and pastors and you and I will notice those we once ignored. It's so that we will befriend sinners who are without hope and without God. It's so that we will share with them the good news of Jesus Christ's substitutionary sacrifice on the cross. It's so that someday those lost souls might turn from their sins and trust in the Savior's death and resurrection on their behalf. And then, there will be some serious rejoicing—on earth and in heaven (Luke 15:10)!

Mark, thank you for writing *The Gospel and Personal Evangelism.* Thank you even more for your compelling example of compassion for the lost and for your faithfulness to proclaim Jesus Christ and him crucified. May there be many gospel conversations and abundant evangelistic fruit as a result of this book.

I'm looking forward to our next lunch together, my friend. Let's walk to Subway.

C.J. Mahaney
Sovereign Grace Ministries

Introduction
An Amazing Story

Let me tell you an amazing story about a person you want to be like. And please hang in there through some of the details. I can't tell stories any other way.

John Harper was born in a Christian home in Glasgow, Scotland, in 1872. When he was about fourteen years old, he became a Christian himself, and from that time on, he began to tell others about Christ. At seventeen years of age, he began to preach, going down the streets of his village and pouring out his soul in passionate pleading for men to be reconciled to God.

After five or six years of toiling on street corners preaching the gospel and working in the mill during the day, Harper was taken in by the Reverend E. A. Carter of Baptist Pioneer Mission in London. This set Harper free to devote his whole time and energy to the work so dear to his heart—evangelism. Soon, in September 1896, Harper started his own church. This church, which he began with just twenty-five members, numbered over five hundred by the time he left thirteen years later. During this time he had been both married and widowed. Before he lost his wife, God blessed Harper with a beautiful little girl named Nana.

Harper's life was an eventful one. He almost drowned several times. When he was two-and-a-half years of age, he fell into a well but was resuscitated by his mother. At the age of twenty-six, he was swept out to sea by a reverse current and barely survived. And at thirty-two he faced death on a leaking ship in the Mediterranean. If anything, these brushes with death simply seemed to confirm John Harper in his zeal for evangelism, which marked him out for the rest of the days of his life.

While pastoring his church in London, Harper continued his fervent and faithful evangelism. In fact, he was such a zealous evangelist that the Moody Church in Chicago asked him to come over to America for a series of meetings. He did, and they went well. A few years later, Moody Church asked him if he would come back again. And so it was that Harper boarded a ship one day with a second-class ticket at Southampton, England, for the voyage to America.

Harper's wife had died just a few years before, and he had with him his only child, Nana, age six. What happened after this we know mainly from two sources. One is Nana, who died in 1986 at the age of eighty. She remembered being woken up by her father a few nights into their journey. It was about midnight, and he said that the ship they were on had struck an iceberg. Harper told Nana that another ship was just about there to rescue them, but, as a precaution, he was going to put her in a lifeboat with an older cousin, who had accompanied them. As for Harper, he would wait until the other ship arrived.

The rest of the story is a tragedy well known. Little Nana and her cousin were saved. But the ship they were on was the *Titanic*. The only way we know what happened to John Harper after is because, in a prayer meeting in Hamilton, Ontario, some months later, a young Scotsman stood up in tears and told the extraordinary story of how he was converted. He explained that he had been on the *Titanic* the night it struck the iceberg. He had clung to a piece of floating debris in the freezing waters. "Suddenly," he said, "a wave brought a man near, John Harper. He, too, was holding a piece of wreckage.

"He called out, 'Man, are you saved?'

"'No, I am not,' I replied.

"He shouted back, 'Believe on the Lord Jesus Christ, and thou shalt be saved.'

"The waves bore [Harper] away, but a little later, he was washed back beside me again. 'Are you saved now?' he called out.

"'No,' I answered. 'Believe on the Lord Jesus Christ and thou shalt be saved.'

"Then losing his hold on the wood, [Harper] sank. And there, alone in the night with two miles of water under me, I trusted Christ as my savior. I am John Harper's last convert."[1]

Now for something completely different—my life story as an evangelist. I am no John Harper. Sometimes I'm a reluctant evangelist. In fact, not only am I sometimes a reluctant evangelist, sometimes I'm no evangelist at all. There have been times of wrestling: "Should I talk to him?" Normally a very forward person, even by American standards, I can get quiet, respectful of the other people's space. Maybe I'm sitting next to someone on an airplane (in which case I've already left that person little space!); maybe it's someone talking to me about some other matter. It may be a family member I've known for years, or a person I've never met before; but, whoever it is, the person becomes for me, at that moment, a witness-stopping, excuse-inspiring spiritual challenge.

If there is a time in the future when God reviews all of our missed evangelistic opportunities, I fear that I could cause more than a minor delay in eternity.

If you are anything like me when it comes to evangelism

(and many people are), then let me encourage you for picking up this little book at all. It is meant to be an encouragement, a clarification, an instruction, a rebuke, and a challenge all rolled up into several short chapters. My prayer is that because of the time you spend reading this book, more people will hear the good news of Jesus Christ.

Isn't it amazing that we have trouble sharing such wonderful news? Who would mind telling a friend that they held a winning lottery ticket? What doctor wouldn't want to tell their patient that the tests came back negative (which, of course, is a good thing)? Who wouldn't be honored by a phone call from the White House saying that the president wanted to meet with him?

So why is it, when we have the best news in the world, that we are so slow to tell it to others? Sometimes our problem may be any one of a long list of excuses. Perhaps we don't know the gospel well enough—or we don't think we do. Maybe we think it's someone else's job, the work of a minister or a missionary. Maybe we just don't really know how to go about it. Or perhaps we *think* we are evangelizing when we really are not.

Let's say that we are faithful with evangelism, but what do we do if the one we are evangelizing gets upset or even gets mad at us? On the other hand, what do we do if it works, if someone "prays the prayer" with us, or at least says that she wants to be a Christian?

And one more question Christians often ask about evangelism: is it okay if I don't really want to evangelize but simply do it out of guilt? I know it's not best, but is it at least okay? These are some of the questions we want to answer. In addition to those, I want to look at a few other questions about sharing the good news: Why don't we evangelize? What is the gospel? Who should evangelize? How should we evangelize? What *isn't* evangelism? What should we do after we evangelize? Why should we evangelize? In sum, we discuss in this book the best news that there has ever been, and how we should share that news.

God has established who and how we should evangelize. God himself is at the heart of the *evangel*—the good news we are spreading. And we should evangelize, ultimately, because of God. All we are doing in this book is connecting some of those dots in our thinking, and, I pray, in our speaking, as well.

Our answers to these questions are not all completely distinct. They weave in and out and one influences the other, but they each provide a separate viewpoint from which to see and understand this great biblical topic of evangelism. To answer these questions, we will look through all the New Testament, from that epicenter of evangelism—the book of Acts—to the Gospels and the letters.

Of course, this little book can't answer all the questions there are about evangelism (because I can't answer all the questions!), but my prayer is that by considering them, you'll find that you can be more understanding and obedient in evangelism. I can't promise you'll become another John Harper (I haven't yet), but we can all become more faithful.

I also pray that as you come to evangelize more, you will help your church to develop a culture of evangelism. What do I mean by a culture of evangelism? I mean an expectation that Christians will share the gospel with others, talk about doing that, pray about it, and regularly plan and work together to help each other evangelize. We want evangelism to be normal—in our own lives and in our churches.

It's to this end I've written this book, and I pray it's to this end you're reading it.

1

Why *Don't* We Evangelize?

A. T. Robertson was a famous Bible teacher and a beloved seminary lecturer. He was also known as a tough professor. At the time, students would stand in class and recite from memory long passages from their assigned books. Sometimes it went well for students; other times it didn't. Once after a particularly poor performance, Dr. Robertson said to a student, "Well, excuse me, brother, but all I can do for you is pray for you and flunk you."[1]

"Flunk" is a word we don't use much anymore. It's a hard, sharp, inflexible kind of word. But it's probably a good word to use to quickly summarize how most of us have done in obeying the call to evangelize. Jesus says to tell all nations the good news, but we haven't. Jesus calls people to be fishers of men, but we prefer to watch. Peter says to always be ready to give a reason for the hope that we have, but we are not. Solomon says he who wins souls is wise, but we flunk.

But if you're anything like me, you're probably not quite so blunt about your failures in evangelism. You've altered your mental records. In fact, even at the time you're not witnessing, you're busy spinning, justifying, rationalizing, and explaining to your conscience why it was really wise and faithful and kind and obedient *not* to share the gospel with a particular person at that time and in that situation.

Throughout the rest of this chapter, we want to consider some of the most common excuses we use to justify our non-evangelism. Generally, those excuses just come into our minds, save us from having certain conversations, and then quickly pass by. In this chapter, we want to slow down our excuses and keep them quiet for just a moment so that we can talk to each of them. Of course, there are thousands more excuses than those listed here, but these are some particularly popular ones. First we'll consider five especially common ones. Then we'll look at a few excuses that are rooted in unbelievers, those who are refusing the gospel news we try to bring. Finally, we'll consider the excuses that are more about ourselves, and we'll see what we can do about them.

Basic Excuse 1: "I don't know their language."

Now, a language barrier is an impressive excuse. And it's got to be about the best one in this chapter. If you're sitting next to people who only speak Chinese or French, you don't have much of an opportunity to share any news with them, let alone news about Christ and their own soul. Of course, you can work to learn another language and so be able to share with many other people. You can keep around Bibles or evangelistic literature in other languages to give away as you have opportunity. But ever since the Tower of Babel, "I don't know" has been one of the most legitimate excuses we could imagine. Paul warns the Corinthians of the uselessness of speaking words that are unintelligible to someone (1 Cor. 14:10–11, 16, 23). After all, the whole point of our using words is to be understood!

Basic Excuse 2: "Evangelism is illegal."

In some places, evangelism *is* illegal. There are countries around the world in which tyrannies of darkness reign. They might be atheistic or Muslim, secular or even "Christian" (in name). But in many countries, sharing the evangelical gospel is forbidden. And it certainly is not to be believed by people who are not already confessing Christians! In such countries, you can usually go out and evangelize—once. It's the second or third time that might be prevented by social pressure, or laws, or jails, or guns. Not many of us reading this book are probably in that position, though.

Basic Excuse 3: "Evangelism could cause problems at work."

Even in countries where evangelism is legally allowed, many of us have jobs for which employers are paying us to get a certain amount of work done, and they have a legitimate expectation. During those work hours, it may be that our evangelism distracts people, or reduces our productivity, or does other things that can cause our employers valid concern. We certainly don't want the sharing of the gospel to bring us or the gospel into disrepute for any reason other than a disagreement with the message itself. We understand that everyone is, by nature, at enmity with God; but we simply don't want to give people other reasons to oppose our evangel. We don't want our evangelism to stand in the way of the *evangel*—the good news.

Basic Excuse 4: "Other things seem more urgent."

There is so much else to do in any given day. We've got to care for our families and plan for our weekend. The job has to be done, and the bills have to be paid. Studies, cooking, cleaning, shopping, returning calls, writing e-mails, reading, praying—I could go on and on about all the good things we need to do. And many of these things are time-sensitive. If I have a misunderstanding with my wife, I need to take care of that immediately. If the baby is crying, I need to get her home now. If the paper is due tomorrow, I've got to get the writing done right away. If we've got no food for tonight, I've got to do some shopping and cooking now. It is legitimate for me to make and fulfill many commitments in life other than evangelism. But do our other commitments sometimes become so numerous—or do we interpret them so—as to leave no time for evangelism? If we are too busy for that, what things are we managing to make time for?

Basic Excuse 5: "I don't know non-Christians."

Isolation from unbelievers may be the most common excuse for a lack of evangelism. This is the excuse of choice for mature Christians. When I'm honestly reflecting on my own life, I see that I have fairly few significant relationships with non-Christians. I'm a pastor. I'm not around non-Christians much as part of my job. I am busy writing sermons, counseling, planning, training other Christians, returning phone calls—even writing a book on evangelism! I'm generally unavailable to people except for my church members during the day or my family in the evening. I'm really absorbed with Christian relationships, and I think that I'm called to be.

But in cases like mine, how does evangelism fit in? If you're a young mother at home with her children, or an older Christian, retired and not easily able to build new relationships, then you, too, know something of this challenge. If you're a new Christian, you've probably been advised (wisely) to build new, significant friendships with Christians. And if you've been a Christian for a while, then you're probably busy with service in the church and spending your time discipling younger Christians. One of the best decisions we can make is to pray and talk with a Christian friend about how we can legitimately fulfill our roles in the church, in our family, and in our job while also getting to know and speak with non-Christians.

Excuses Concerning Them

Another set of excuses has to do with problems you and I think that others will have with our witnessing to them. How many times have I had these more subtle and advanced excuses assemble in my mind as I'm thinking about sharing the gospel with someone? "People don't want to hear." "They won't be interested." "They probably already know the gospel." "It probably won't work. I doubt they'll believe." I don't think about how powerful the gospel is. I get myself in a wrongly hopeless mindset.

Of course, I should consider how faithless all this is. As Paul said to the Corinthians, "Who makes you different from anyone else? What do you have that you did not receive?" (1 Cor. 4:7). Why do we think that *we* would respond to the gospel, but someone else wouldn't? Haven't you found that God saves some of the most unlikely converts? If you aren't sure about this, consider some friends you've seen converted. Consider your own conversion. Jonathan Edwards called one account of the Great Awakening *A Narrative of Surprising Conversions*. Of course, in one sense, all conversions are surprising: enemies are loved, the alienated are adopted, those who should be punished inherit eternal life instead. But it is exactly this radical, surprising nature of conversion that should encourage us in our evangelism. God may save anyone. And the more unlikely it appears, the more glory, we might even reason, he gets to himself when it happens!

The Heart of the Matter: Plan to Stop Not Evangelizing

Here we are getting down closer to the heart of most of our non-evangelism. What's going on with us when we don't evangelize? Let's think about twelve steps we can take: pray, plan, accept, understand, be faithful, risk, prepare, look, love, fear, stop, and consider.

1) Pray. I think many times we don't evangelize because we undertake everything in our own power. We attempt to leave God out of it. We forget that it is his will and pleasure for his gospel to be known. He wants sinners saved. Simply put, we don't pray for opportunities to share the gospel, so how surprised should we be when they don't come? If you're not evangelizing because you think you lack opportunities, pray and be amazed as God answers your prayers.

2) Plan. As we've already considered, sometimes we don't evangelize because we think, "I'm busy with other good things. Those other things are legitimate ways for me to spend my time. So I just don't have time for evangelism right now. When my health improves . . . after my paper is due . . . when my son is in school . . . when my husband retires . . . when I get that promotion . . . when she's in a better mood, then," we say, "I'll share the gospel with her." To fight such excuse making, we can plan to make time to build relationships or to put ourselves in positions where we know we'll be able to talk with non-Christians. We plan for so many less important things; why not plan for our evangelism?

3) Accept. We have to accept that this is our job. We'll consider this more in chapter 3, but for now, let's just acknowledge that sometimes we don't evangelize because we think it's not our job. It's the job of preachers, we think, or someone else who is trained and paid for it. But if we are going to evangelize, we have to realize and admit how we've been dodging our duty and adjust ourselves to accept responsibility for evangelism. We might be the closest Christians to a particular unbeliever. Maybe he has a Christian uncle or aunt, friend, or employee who has been praying for him. Maybe we are the answer to those prayers. We must accept, we may accept, we get to accept the wonderful role that God has for us as evangelists in others' lives!

4) Understand. Part of our failure to evangelize comes from a lack of understanding. God uses not so much gifts for evangelism (though there is a biblical gift of evangelism) but the faithfulness of thousands and millions of Christians who would never say evangelism is their gift. Your conclusion that you are not gifted for a particular task does not absolve you of responsibility to obey. You may conclude that evangelism is not your gift, but it is still your duty. Not having the gift of mercy in no way excuses us from being merciful. All Christians are to exercise mercy; some will be particularly gifted to do this in special ways at certain times, but all are to be merciful. So with evangelism. God may unusually bless and own a Peter and a Philip, a Whitefield and a Spurgeon, a Hudson Taylor and an Adoniram Judson, but he calls all of us to share the good news.

5) Be Faithful. Perhaps we need to rebalance our allegiances. Maybe we are too polite to be faithful to God in this area. Maybe we are more concerned about people's response than God's glory. Maybe we are more concerned about their feelings than God's. God does not like having his truth suppressed, and that's what the non-Christian is doing (Rom. 1:18). Good manners are no excuse for unfaithfulness to God, but we have, too often, used them so.

6) Risk. Related to being faithful is being willing to risk. Let's obey, even when we are not exactly sure of the response. Maybe you don't evangelize sometimes because you're shy. You don't really enjoy talking to others that much, especially about things that may upset them. It seems tiring and dangerous. Maybe you would rather let someone else, someone who seems more comfortable, do the evangelizing. But could you invite unbelievers to a meeting where they will hear the gospel? Can you share with them a useful book or a story from your own life? Can you befriend them so that you may be able more naturally in the future to share the gospel with them? We must be willing to risk in order to evangelize.

7) **Prepare.** Sometimes we don't evangelize because we think we are unprepared or ill-equipped. Maybe we don't know how to transition the conversation. Or perhaps we think that in our ignorance we'll fail at this and actually do spiritual harm to the person by discrediting the gospel in their eyes. We fear our ignorance. We think that it's up to us to make the gospel seem sensible to them or to answer all their questions. And, so, having inflated these expectations, we decide we can't meet them and so neglect evangelism. Instead, we could prepare ourselves by knowing the gospel, working on our own humility, and studying more. Just as we might plan to have time, so we might prepare to be able to use the opportunity well when it comes.

8) **Look.** Have you ever prayed for something and then been surprised when it comes? I know I have. And I guess that means I really must not have been expecting God to answer that prayer request. It may be the same with my evangelism. Maybe I've prayed for opportunities but then not really looked for them. Perhaps I've been careless when they've come.

The way I've been careless can vary. Sometimes I don't see the opportunities because I'm busy. Evangelism can, after all, be time consuming and inconvenient. Or maybe I'm too tired. Perhaps I've used up all my energy on entertaining myself, or working, or on everything other than this non-Christian whom I could talk to. And therefore I don't even notice the opportunity.

Maybe my neglect of opportunities is more habitual. Maybe I'm lazy, caring more that I not be hassled or hurried than that this person hears the gospel. Maybe, when it comes right down to it, I'm simply selfish. I don't see the opportunities because I'm unwilling to be inconvenienced. I guess that means that I am, finally, apathetic. My blindness to God's provision is voluntary. I don't consider the reality and finality of death, judgment, and hell. So I don't notice the reality of the person and their plight before me. We must not only close our eyes in prayer for opportunities, but we must then open our eyes to see them.

9) **Love.** We are called to love others. We share the gospel because we love people. And we don't share the gospel because we don't love people. Instead, we wrongly fear them. We don't want to cause awkwardness. We want their respect, and after all, we figure, if we try to share the gospel with them, we'll look foolish! And so we are quiet. We protect our pride at the cost of their souls. In the name of not wanting to look weird, we are content to be complicit in their being lost. As one friend said, "I don't want to be the stereotypical Christian on a plane."

That attitude too often characterizes me. My heart is cold to other people. I have a distorted self-love and a deficient love for others. And just to drive this home, as I've been writing this, a non-Christian friend called and wanted to talk to me. We chatted for about thirty minutes, the whole time during which I was impatient to get back to writing this book on evangelism! Aargh! Wretched man that I am! Who shall deliver me from this body of indifference? If we would evangelize more, we must love people more.

10) **Fear.** We should also fear. But our fear should be directed not to man but to God. When we don't share the gospel, we are essentially refusing to live in the fear of the Lord. We are not regarding him or his will as the final and ultimate rule of our actions. To fear God is to love him. When the One who is our all-powerful creator and judge is also our merciful redeemer and savior, then we have found the perfect object for the entire devotion of our heart. And that devotion will lead

us to share this good news about him with others. We should pray that God will grow in us a greater love and fear of him.

11) Stop. We should stop blaming God. We should stop excusing ourselves from evangelism on the basis that God is sovereign. We should not conclude from his omnipotence that our obedience is therefore pointless. We should instead read from the Word that God will call a great number to himself from every tribe, tongue, and nation, which will encourage us in evangelism. It encouraged Paul in Corinth when he was discouraged (see Acts 18). Again, if you will realize that conversion always accompanies proclaiming the gospel and the Spirit's work, then you will stop trying to do the Spirit's work, and you will give yourself to proclaiming the gospel. Just because we don't know everything doesn't mean we don't know anything! We can't answer all the questions of how God's sovereignty and human responsibility fit together, but we can certainly believe that they do. It was Paul who wrote one of the clearest biblical passages about God's sovereignty (Romans 9) and then went on to write one of the most pointed biblical passages about man's responsibility in evangelism (Romans 10). He certainly believed both these things to be true. So who are we to blame God for our sinful silence?

12) Consider. The writer of Hebrews said, "Consider him who endured such opposition from sinful men, so that you will not grow weary and lose heart" (Heb. 12:3). When we don't sufficiently consider what God has done for us in Christ—the high cost of it, what it means, and what Christ's significance is—we lose the heart to evangelize. Our hearts grow cold, our minds grow smaller (more taken up with passing concerns), and our lips fall silent. Consider that God has loved us as he has. Consider that God is glorified by our telling others of this amazing love of his. And consider that instead of gossiping about God's goodness and the gospel, we engage in a conspiracy of silence. We reveal ourselves as being cold to God's glory. If we would be more faithful in evangelism, we should fuel the flame of love toward God within us, and the flame of gratitude and of hope. A fire so enflamed by God will have no trouble igniting our tongue. As Jesus said, "Out of the overflow of the heart the mouth speaks" (Matt. 12:34). How much evangelism do we find flowing out of our mouths? What does that suggest about our love for God?

For that matter, why should we so love God? That brings us to consider what exactly this message is that we want to share. What is it that would so fire our hearts? That's what we want to consider in the next chapter.

2

What Is the Gospel?

My friends know that I enjoy words, so sometimes for Christmas I'll get calendars with interesting stories or word facts. I can't remember on which calendar I read the following account, but I was so struck by it, I made a note of it. I don't know if it's true, but it's a great illustration of the importance of getting your story right.

According to this account, a little over a hundred years ago the editor of an English newspaper opened a copy of his paper—after it was already for sale—only to find in it a most embarrassing, unintentional typographical conflation of two stories, one about a patented pig-killing and sausage-making machine, and the other about a gathering in honor of a local clergyman, the Reverend Doctor Mudge, at which he was presented with a gold-headed cane. A portion of it read as follows:

> Several of Rev. Dr. Mudge's friends called upon him yesterday, and after a conversation the unsuspecting pig was seized by the hind leg, and slid along a beam until he reached the hot-water tank. . . . Thereupon he came forward and said that there were times when the feelings overpowered one, and for that reason he would not attempt to do more than thank those around him for the manner in which such a huge animal was cut into fragments was simply astonish-

ing. The doctor concluded his remarks, when the machine seized him and, in less time than it takes to write it, the pig was cut into fragments and worked up into a delicious sausage. The occasion will be long remembered by the doctor's friends as one of the most delightful of their lives. The best pieces can be procured for tenpence a pound, and we are sure that those who have sat so long under his ministry will rejoice that he has been treated so handsomely.

Christianity is all about news. It is all about the good news, really the best news the world has ever heard. And yet that news—far more important than the story about the Reverend Doctor Mudge or the sausage machine—is often every bit as scrambled and confused. That which passes for the gospel too often becomes a very thin veneer spread lightly over our culture's values, becoming shaped and formed to its contours rather than to the truth about God. The real story, the real message, becomes lost.

This idea of the good news isn't some later Christian packaging scheme. Jesus Christ talked about the good news, and when he did, he reached back to the language of the prophecies of Isaiah hundreds of years earlier (Isa. 52:7; 61:1). Whatever Jesus may have said in Aramaic, the way the Christians, and even his own disciples, remembered it in Greek was with this word *evangel*—literally, good news.

Well, what exactly *is* this good news? In this chapter, we want to try to set the story straight; we want to get the news right. What is the message that we Christians have to tell? Is it that "I'm okay" or "God is love"? Is it that "Jesus is my friend" or "I should live right"? What is the good news of Jesus Christ?

The Good News Is Not Simply That We Are Okay

You may have heard of the book title of almost forty years ago now, *I'm OK, You're OK*.[1] Some people seem to think that Christianity is fundamentally a religious therapy session, where we sit around trying to help each other feel good about ourselves. The pews are couches. The preacher asks questions. The text to be expounded is your inner self. And yet, when we have finished plumbing our inner depths, why is it that we so often feel empty? Or even dirty? Is there something about us and our lives that is incomplete or even wrong?

I remember hearing one celebrity being interviewed on television after the death of a close friend. Weeping, this celebrity exclaimed, "Why does everyone I love die?" Yes, why indeed. The Bible utterly rejects the idea that we are okay, that the human condition is just fine, that everyone is merely in need of accepting their current condition, their finitude, or their imperfections, or that we simply need to begin to look on the bright side of it.

The Bible teaches that in our first parents, Adam and Eve, we have all been seduced into disobeying God. We are therefore not righteous and on good terms with God. In fact, our sin is so serious that Jesus taught that we need a new birth (John 3), and Paul taught that we need to be created again (1 Corinthians 15). As we find in Ephesians 2, we are *dead* in our sins and transgressions.

You know what transgressions are—they are sins simply represented as going across a boundary. In our day and age, Michel Foucault would live, like the Marquis de Sade before him, in order to transgress boundaries. And so there is some thought that Foucault deliberately sought to infect others with the AIDS virus as he himself contracted it and died through it. The bathhouses of San Francisco became the place where Foucault not only transgressed the boundaries of respect for sexuality but also of respect for life itself. Transgressions. Crossings over the line.

Our transgressions may not seem so blatant and offensive, but they are surely no less deadly for our relationship with God. Paul says in Romans 6:23 that "the wages of sin is death." We understand more of why and how that is the case by turning to the letter of James. James said, "For whoever keeps the whole law and yet stumbles at just one point is guilty of breaking all of it. For he who said, 'Do not commit adultery,' also said, 'Do not murder.' If you do not commit adultery but do commit murder, you have become a lawbreaker" (James 2:10–11).

Notice the seriousness of each sin. The point James is making is that the laws of God are not simply external statutes passed by some congress in heaven that God enforces. The law of God is the expression of God's own character. To break out of this law, to live against it, is to live against God.

If my wife sends me to the store with specific instructions to get a particular item and I come back without having gotten it and with no good excuse (such as "They were out of it" or "I couldn't find it" or "We shouldn't get this"), but simply having decided not to get it, that will reflect on our relationship.

The Bible presents God not simply as our creator but as our jealous lover. He wants us—every part of us. For us to think that we can disregard him sometimes, to set aside his ways when it suits us, is to show that we haven't understood the nature of the relationship at all. So, you see, we can't claim to be believers and yet knowingly, repeatedly, happily break God's law.

But this is our state. We have crossed over the bounds that God has rightly set for our lives. We have contradicted him in both the letter and the spirit of his instructions to us. And so we not only feel guilt, but we actually are guilty before God. We are not only conflicted in ourselves; we are actually in conflict with God. We break God's laws again and again. And we do this because we are, says Ephesians 2, dead in our sins and transgressions.

Now all of this may seem to be too grim to have much at all to do with anything called "the good news." But there is no doubt that an accurate understanding of where we are now is essential to getting to where we need to be. One of the early stages of becoming a Christian is, I think, realizing that our problems aren't fundamentally that we have messed up our own lives, or have simply failed to reach our full potential, but that we have sinned against God. And so it begins to dawn on us that we are rightly the objects of God's wrath and his judgment, and that we deserve death, separation from God, and spiritual alienation from him now and even forever.

This is what the theologians call depravity. It is the death that deserves death.

Do you see the reason that all of these wrongs are so tragic? These sins are committed against a perfect, holy, loving God. And they are committed by creatures made in his image.

True Christianity is realistic about the dark side of our world, our life, our nature, our heart. But true Christianity is not finally pessimistic or morally indifferent, encouraging us to merely settle in and accept the cold, hard truth. No. The news that we, as Christians, have to bring is so great, so tremendous, not only because our depravity is so pervasive and our sin so widespread, but also because God's plans for us are so different, so wonderful.

And when we begin to realize it, we become thankful for the fact that Christianity is not finally about anesthetizing us to life's pain, or even about waking us up to it and teaching us to live with it. It is about teaching us to live with a transforming longing, with a growing faith, with a sure and certain hope of what's to come.

The Good News Is Not Simply That God Is Love

Other times we may hear the gospel simply represented as the message that God is love. Now, this one is sort of like the Oklahoma newspaper headline that read, "Cold Weather Causes Temperatures to Drop." It's not that it's not true; it's just that it's so obvious that something is missing or left out.

That "God is love" is certainly true. It's even in the Bible! "God is love" (1 John 4:8). But there is a danger in simply saying so as if it is self-evident.

Maybe we get a little sense of what this love is when, as parents, we tell our children that, for some good reason about which we are aware, they can't do something they want to do. And what is an oft-heard response? "If you really *loved* me, you'd *let* me." Now that's just plain wrong! But it's a falsehood that can be as subtle as it is significant. Love doesn't always let. Indeed, sometimes love prevents, and sometimes love punishes.

If we say that God is love, what are we thinking that his love must look like?

And furthermore, is love all that the Bible says that God is? Doesn't the Bible say that God is a Spirit? How does a Spirit love? Doesn't the Bible say that God is holy? How does a Holy Spirit love? Doesn't the Bible say that God is unique, that there is none other like him? How does the only perfect Holy Spirit in the universe love? How can you know if he doesn't tell you? Can you surmise it, figure it out, assume it from your own experience, or chart out how it would be from your own heart? John Calvin said:

> It is plain that no man can arrive at the true knowledge of himself, without having first contemplated the divine character, and then descended to the consideration of his own. For, such is the native pride of us all, we invariably

esteem ourselves righteous, innocent, wise and holy, till we are convinced by clear proofs, of our unrighteousness, turpitude, folly and impurity. But we are never thus convinced, while we confine our attention to ourselves, and regard not the Lord, who is the only standard by which this judgment ought to be formed.[2]

Among other important things to note is this: God reveals himself as the God who requires holiness of all who would be in loving relationship with him. As the Bible says, "Without holiness, no one will see the Lord" (Heb. 12:14). It is only in the context of understanding something of God's character, of his righteousness and perfection, that we begin to understand the tremendous nature of saying that God truly is love, and his love has a depth, texture, fullness, and beauty to it that we, in our present state, can only begin to wonder at.

The Good News Is Not Simply That Jesus Wants to Be Our Friend

Other times the gospel message is represented to us rather simply as "Jesus wants to be our friend" or, as a variation of that, "Jesus wants to be our example." But the Christian gospel is not a matter of mere self-help or even of a great example or a relationship to be cultivated. There is a real past to be dealt with. Real sins have been committed. Real guilt has been incurred. And so what is to be done? What will our holy God do? Even if he, in his love, wants a people for his own, how will he have them without sacrificing his own holiness?

Did he simply come in the flesh to teach us that our sins are no big deal, that he's just going to forgive and forget? What would that do to the morality of God? What would that do to the character of the One who is said to love us?

What does Jesus want? What did he come to do? What is

amazing, when we study the gospels, is that we find that Jesus chose to die. This is what Jesus presented as the center of his ministry. Not teaching or even being an example, but, as he said, "The Son of Man did not come to be served, but to serve, and to give his life as a ransom for many" (Mark 10:45). Jesus himself taught that this choice of his to glorify the Father by his death on the cross was central to his ministry. It's not surprising, then, that the center and focus of all four Gospel accounts is Christ's crucifixion.

But what does it mean? And why would something that seems such a horrifying event be the focus of anything called "good news"?

The New Testament began to explain this event even before it happened in the words of Jesus himself. Jesus wove together two strands of Old Testament prophecy (Mark 8:27–38), which, to the best of my knowledge, had not previously been united. Here Jesus presented himself as a combination of the Son of Man (Daniel 7) and the Suffering Servant (Isaiah 53).

The apostles clearly learned from Jesus how they were to understand his death on the cross; and to teach Christians about this, the Holy Spirit has inspired various images in the New Testament that convey the reality to us: Jesus as a sacrifice, a redemption, a reconciliation, a legal justification, a military victory, and a propitiation.

None of this language in the New Testament refers to something potential, a mere possibility, or an option; rather, each image refers to something that actually accomplishes its end or purpose. So, for example, how can we say that God and sinners are reconciled if these "reconciled sinners" were then cast into hell? Or what kind of propitiation would it be if God's wrath was not assuaged, or what kind of redemption if the hostages were not set free? The point with all these images is that the benefit envisioned has not merely been made available; it has been secured not by the mere teaching ministry of Christ but by his death and resurrection.

There's no getting around the fact that the center of Christ's ministry was his death on the cross, and the heart of that death was God's certainly and effectively dealing with the claims of both his own love and justice. So much of this—blood, purchase, victory—comes together in the magnificence of the final vision given by God to John:

> Then one of the elders said to me, "Do not weep! See, the Lion of the tribe of Judah, the Root of David, has triumphed. He is able to open the scroll and its seven seals." Then I saw a Lamb, looking as if it had been slain, standing in the center of the throne, encircled by the four living creatures and the elders. . . . He came and took the scroll from the right hand of him who sat on the throne. And when he had taken it, the four living creatures and the twenty-four elders fell down before the Lamb. Each one had a harp and they were holding golden bowls full of incense, which are the prayers of the saints. And they sang a new song:
>
> "You are worthy to take the scroll
>   and to open its seals,
> because you were slain,
>   and with your blood you purchased men for God
>   from every tribe and language and people and
>   nation." (Rev. 5:5–9)

Christ isn't just our friend. To call him supremely that is to damn him with faint praise. He is our friend, but he is so much more! By his death on the cross Christ has become the lamb that was slain for us, our redeemer, the one who has made peace between us and God, who has taken our guilt on himself, who has conquered our most deadly enemies and has assuaged the personal, just wrath of God.

The Good News Is Not That We Should Live Rightly

Mistaking the gospel for "right living" is one more common error. Sometimes people think that the news, the message of the Bible, is simply that we should live moral lives. Christianity is sometimes presented as nothing more than virtues—public and private. Christians are thought to be simply about *doing* religious things, such as baptism, and communion, and going to church. The Christian life is nothing more than obeying the Ten Commandments and the Golden Rule, reading our Bibles, and praying. Being Christian means building up the community, giving to others, contributing to soup kitchens, and preserving historical buildings rather than making parking lots.

But as startling as it may be to those who think this way, the biblical gospel is not fundamentally about our love or our power. To be a Christian is not merely to live in love, or to live by the power of positive thinking, or to do anything that we can do ourselves. The gospel calls for a more radical response than any of these things allow for. The gospel, you see, is not simply an additive that comes to make our already good lives better. No! The gospel is a message of wonderful good news that comes to those who realize their just desperation before God.

So what response is called for? What is it you should do when your own sense of need, your understanding of God and of Jesus Christ, all begin to come together like this? God calls us to repent of our sins and to rely on Christ alone.

We find both repentance and faith in the New Testament, and often they occur together. As Paul met with the leaders of the church in Ephesus, a meeting which is recounted in Acts 20, he summarized his message this way: "I have declared to both Jews and Greeks that they must turn to God in repentance and have faith in our Lord Jesus" (Acts 20:21). This is the message that Paul and other Christians preached throughout the New Testament.

Once people have heard the truth about their sin and God's holiness, God's love in Christ, and Christ's death and resurrection for our justification, the message calls out for response. And what is that response? Is it to walk down an aisle? Is it to fill out a card or to lift up a hand? Is it to make an appointment to see the preacher or to decide to be baptized and join the church? While any of those things may be involved, none is absolutely necessary. The response to this good news is, as Paul preached, to repent and believe.

Where did Paul and the other authors of the New Testament get this message? If you turn to the first chapter of Mark's Gospel, you'll find out. They got it from Jesus, who called out, "Repent and believe the good news!" (Mark 1:15). The response to this news is believing and repenting.

We must honestly think the gospel is true. But there is more to saving belief than that. You can believe, for example, that the Angel Falls in Venezuela are nearly twenty times higher than Niagara Falls, that a spider's web applied to a bleeding wound helps the blood to clot, that the inhabitants of Iceland read more books per person per year than the inhabitants of any other country, or that Sir Christopher Wren had only six months' training as an architect. But none of these "believings" are what Jesus meant in Mark 1 when he called out for people to believe.

Saving belief is not mere mental assent, but a believing in—a living in—the knowledge of that news. It is a leaning on, a relying on. We must come to grips with the fact that we are unable to satisfy God's demands on us, no matter how morally we try to live. We don't want to end up trusting a little in ourselves and a little in God; we want to realize that we are to rely on God fully, to trust in Christ alone for our salvation.

And such a true believing and relying makes a difference and so demands not only faith but also repentance.

Repentance and this kind of belief, or faith, or reliance, are really two sides of the same coin. It's not like you can go for the basic model (belief) and add repentance at a later point when you want to get really holy. No! Repent is what you do if you really start thinking this way and believing Jesus with your life. Any purported belief without change is nothing but a base counterfeit. As J. C. Ryle said, "There is a common, worldly kind of Christianity in this day, which many have, and think they have enough—a cheap Christianity which offends nobody, and requires no sacrifice—which costs nothing, and is worth nothing."[3]

The repentance that Jesus demands is connected with believing this news, because if it's really "news," it's no surprise that you change your mind when you hear it. The word for "repent" is *metanoia* and means literally "to change your mind."

Real Christianity is never simply an addition to, or merely a cultivation of, something that has always been there. Instead, it is, in some radical sense, an about-face. And it's an about-face all Christians make, but only as a part of their relying on Christ's finished work on the cross. To say you trust without *living* as though you do is not to trust in any biblical sense. And you can see the truth of that from Abraham—the great example of faith—all the way through to Jesus Christ himself.

We change the way we act; we do. But we only change the way we act because we change what we believe. The good news of Christianity has a cognitive content; it's not simply a religious enthusiasm or a deep personal intuition. It is new; it is tidings, the latest. It says something. The gospel is news!

In our church in Washington, I always ask our prospective members to tell me the gospel in one minute or less. How would you do that? What would you say the message is? Here's what I understand the good news to be: the good news is that the one and only God, who is holy, made us in his image to know him. But we sinned and cut ourselves off from him. In his great love, God became a man in Jesus, lived a perfect life, and died on the cross, thus fulfilling the law himself and taking on himself the punishment for the sins of all those who would ever turn and trust in him. He rose again from the dead, showing that God accepted Christ's sacrifice and that God's wrath against us had been exhausted. He now calls us to repent of our sins and to trust in Christ alone for our forgiveness. If we repent of our sins and trust in Christ, we are born again into a new life, an eternal life with God.

Now that's good news.

But is this news too complicated for the average Christian to tell others? We'll think more about that in the next chapter.

3

Who Should Evangelize?

"I couldn't do what you just did."

"What?" I said, honestly clueless.

"Engage that person in conversation like that."

My friend was a strong Christian. He was growing spiritually like a weed. But he was a much younger Christian than I. Plus, he has, I would say, a normally balanced personality, whereas I am an off-the-charts extrovert, which brings blessings and challenges. But the extrovert's ability to talk to a lot of people is one of the pluses.

What isn't one of the pluses is what happened to my friend—he was left feeling that he couldn't evangelize. We went on to have a good conversation about evangelism and about his recent opportunities, but this experience did make me consider the fact that "clergy persons" such as I, whether intentionally or unintentionally, often give off the vibe that evangelism should be left to the professionals. After all, you wouldn't want just anybody to perform surgery on you, would you? You wouldn't want your bank account to be looked after at a gas station, would you? You wouldn't want to assign the keeping of the family checkbook to your second-grade son, would you? "All right then," you feel, "I'm not as eloquent as the man up front. I can't preach like that. I can't answer questions like that."

And then comes the killer conclusion: "I shouldn't share the gospel with others—at least, not much. And when I do, it will be only with close friends . . . and maybe only after a long time . . . and only if they ask me first . . . and only if I've had my quiet time that day. And only if . . ."

Whose job is it to evangelize? There are people in the New Testament who are said to have the gift of evangelism (see Eph. 4:11; Acts 21:8). We know that there are people today who are called evangelists. Sometimes they even set up companies with names like the So-and-So Evangelistic Association. Are they the ones called to spread the good news?

In Acts 4:29 Peter prays, "Now, Lord, consider their threats and enable your servants to speak your word with great boldness." Does that prayer apply only to preachers? Is evangelism really the work of pastors? Paul writes to Timothy, a pastor, to "do the work of an evangelist" (2 Tim. 4:5). Should the called and the equipped become professional evangelists? Are the rest of us to leave it alone for the most part? Are regular church members to be still and remain passive, inviting others to hear only pastors, preachers, speakers, and other trained evangelists? Is our evangelism to be merely inviting people to meetings rather than inviting them directly to Christ?

Is the ordinary Christian doing evangelism like the ordinary employee trying to do the company's accounting? Are we average Christians all to be evangelists, or should we leave that to Bible colleges and seminary graduates?[1]

However difficult this topic of evangelism may be for many of us, it is hard to avoid it without avoiding the Bible. Verses about spreading the good news are all through it. Paul wrote to the Romans, "I am obligated both to Greeks and non-Greeks, both to the wise and the foolish. That is why I am so eager to preach the gospel also to you who are at Rome" (Rom. 1:14–15). But are such statements simply statements of Paul's own calling rather than something that applies to us as well?

Of course, those statements *were* true of Paul. But when we read the New Testament, we don't read of the call to evangelism being limited to Paul, or even to the apostles. It was Jesus himself, in his final commission to his disciples, who taught, "All authority in heaven and on earth has been given to me. Therefore go and make disciples of all nations, baptizing them in the name of the Father and of the Son and of the Holy Spirit, and teaching them to obey everything I have commanded you. And surely I am with you always, to the very end of the age" (Matt. 28:18–20). This is commonly called the Great Commission, which Jesus gave to his disciples, and it would be difficult to overestimate its importance. John Stott concludes from Jesus' words:

> [This] commission . . . is binding upon every member of the whole Church. . . . Every Christian is called to be a witness to Christ in the particular environment in which God has placed him. Further, although the public ministry of the Word is a high office, private witness or personal evangelism has a value which in some respects surpasses even that of preaching, since the message can then be adapted more personally.[2]

These early disciples, having become apostles, took Jesus' Great Commission to heart. They evangelized constantly (see Acts 5:42; 8:25; 13:32; 14:7, 15, 21; 15:35; 16:10; 17:18). But, again, the question some are now asking is, who is supposed to do this today? Is it only preachers or professional religious types?

According to the Bible, all believers have received this commission. In the book of Acts we see glimpses of this universal obedience to the call to evangelize. In Acts 2 we see that all the Christians had God's Spirit poured out upon them. In the Old Testament, such an outpouring was preparation for the work of prophetically giving out God's Word. And so we are not surprised to find, as we continue through the book of Acts, that many people evangelized. We read in Acts 8:1–4:

> On that day a great persecution broke out against the church at Jerusalem, and all except the apostles were scattered throughout Judea and Samaria. Godly men buried Stephen and mourned deeply for him. But Saul began to destroy the church. Going from house to house, he dragged off men and women and put them in prison. Those who had been scattered preached the word wherever they went.

In the same chapter we read the story of Philip, a deacon, doing evangelism (Acts 8:5–12, 26–40); and later we read:

> Now those who had been scattered by the persecution in connection with Stephen traveled as far as Phoenicia, Cyprus and Antioch, telling the message only to Jews. Some of them, however, men from Cyprus and Cyrene, went to Antioch and began to speak to Greeks also, telling them the good news about the Lord Jesus. The Lord's hand was with them, and a great number of people believed and turned to the Lord. (Acts 11:19–21)

It's clear, too, from all the talk of persecution in the New Testament that the earliest Christians didn't try to keep their religion a secret, even though sharing it brought consequences. Paul wrote to the young Thessalonian Christians about their "severe suffering" (1 Thess. 1:6), and he refers to those who were troubling them (2 Thess. 2:5–7). We see this elsewhere in the New Testament also. Even though Christians were suffering because their lives had changed, they continued to speak in order to share the gospel and to explain their new faith.

And then there are Peter's instructions to Christians in 1 Peter 3:15–16:

But in your hearts set apart Christ as Lord. Always be prepared to give an answer to everyone who asks you to give the reason for the hope that you have. But do this with gentleness and respect, keeping a clear conscience, so that those who speak maliciously against your good behavior in Christ may be ashamed of their slander.

We know that Christ himself came to seek and to save what was lost (Luke 15; 19:10). In atoning for sinners Christ is uniquely our savior. In seeking sinners as he did, however, he is our example. So how can we follow Jesus Christ without inviting people to come to Christ? Can we be his disciples and not seek the lost coin, the lost sheep, the lost son? There is a lot of witnessing in the book of Acts. The lost were prayed for and sought after even by those who are not named as apostles, evangelists, or elders.

When Jesus is asked by a lawyer what the most important commandment is, he responds by quoting Deuteronomy 6, an exhortation to love God, and Leviticus 19, an exhortation to "Love your neighbor as yourself" (Mark 12:31). James calls this love the "royal law" (James 2:8). What does such love require of us? It seems to require that what we want for ourselves, we want for those we love, too. If you desire to love God with perfect affection, you will desire that for your neighbor, too. But you are not loving your neighbor as yourself if you're not trying to persuade him toward the greatest and best aspect of your own life—your reconciled relationship with God. If you are a Christian, you are pursuing Christ. You are following him, and you desire him. And you must therefore also desire this highest good for everyone whom you love. It is love itself that requires us to pursue the best for those we love, and that must include sharing the good news of Jesus Christ with them.

Furthermore, every Christian is to live a life that commends the gospel. The love that the New Testament community of believers shared is presented as an integral part of their witness to the world, as we see in John 13:34–35. This love was not shared only among the leaders; it was shared between all Christians. In fact, the outworking of faith through the community of a local church seems to be Jesus' most basic evangelism plan. And it involves all of us.[3] Paul wrote to the Philippian church commanding them to continue holding out the word of life (Phil. 2:16). They would do that by both their lives and their words.

We know that God's intent in establishing the church was to bear witness to himself and to his character. As Paul wrote, "His intent was that now, through the church, the manifold wisdom of God should be made known" (Eph. 3:10). And though Paul says that it was to be made known to the rulers and authorities in heavenly realms, we know from elsewhere in the New Testament that it was also God's plan to make known his character to other people.

Every Christian has a role in making visible the gospel of the invisible God. God's love, supremely, is to be revealed in the church. John Stott commented on this challenge and opportunity:

> The invisibility of God is a great problem. It was already a problem to God's people in Old Testament days. Their pagan neighbors would taunt them, saying, "Where is now your God?" Their gods were visible and tangible, but Israel's God was neither. Today in our scientific culture young people are taught not to believe in anything which is not open to empirical investigation. How then has God solved the problem of his own invisibility? The first answer is of course "in Christ." Jesus Christ is the visible image of the invisible God. John 1:18: "No one has ever seen God, but God the only Son has made him known." "That's wonderful," people say, "but it was 2,000 years ago. Is there no way by

which the invisible God makes himself visible today?" There is. We return to 1 John 4:12: "No one has ever seen God." It is precisely the same introductory statement. But instead of continuing with reference to the Son of God, it continues: "If we love one another, God dwells in us." In other words, the invisible God, who once made himself visible in Christ, now makes himself visible in Christians, *if* we love one another. It is a breathtaking claim. The local church cannot evangelize, proclaiming the gospel of love, if it is not itself a community of love.[4] (Emphasis in original)

One of the main reasons that the local church is to be a community of love is so that others will know the God of love. God made people in his image to know him. The life of the local congregation makes the audible gospel visible. And we must all have a part in that evangelism.

We can all contribute to evangelism simply by building up the local church—helping to organize it or lead it. We may teach and equip. We may provide hospitality and encouragement. We may pray and serve and show mercy and give. But we also all have a responsibility to speak of God and the good news both inside and outside of the church.

Martyn Lloyd-Jones taught, "Evangelism is pre-eminently dependent upon the quality of the Christian life which is known and enjoyed in the church."[5] A striking example of this truth is found in John Bunyan's experience. He recounted it himself in his autobiography, *Grace Abounding to the Chief of Sinners* (by which title he meant himself). Bunyan tells this story:

> One day, the good providence of God did cast me to Bedford, to work on my own calling; and in one of the streets of that town, I came where there were three or four poor women sitting at a door in the sun, and talking about the things of God; and being now willing to hear them discourse, I drew near to hear what they said, for I was now a brisk talker also myself

in the matters of religion, but now I may say, I heard, but I understood not; for they were far above, out of my reach, for their talk was about a new birth, the work of God on their hearts, also how they were convinced of their miserable state by nature; they talked how God had visited their souls with His love in the Lord Jesus, and with what words and promises they had been refreshed, comforted, and supported against the temptations of the devil. Moreover, they reasoned of the suggestions and temptations of Satan in particular; and told to each other by which they had been afflicted, and how they were borne up under his assaults. They also discoursed of their own wretchedness of heart, of their unbelief; and did contemn, slight and abhor their own righteousness, as filthy and insufficient to do them any good.

And methought they spake as if joy did make them speak; they spake with such pleasantness of Scripture language, and with such appearance of grace in all they said, that they were to me as if they had found a new world, as if they were people that dwelt alone, and were not to be reckoned among their neighbours (Num. 23:9).

At this I felt my own heart began to shake, as mistrusting my condition to be naught; for I saw that in all my thoughts about religion and salvation, the new birth did never enter into my mind, neither knew I the comfort of the Word and promise, nor the deceitfulness and treachery of my own wicked heart. As for secret thoughts, I took no notice of them; neither did I understand what Satan's temptations were, nor how they were to be withstood and resisted, etc.

Thus, therefore, when I had heard and considered what they said, I left them, and went about my employment again, but their talk and discourse went with me, also my heart would tarry with them, for I was greatly affected with their words, both because by them I was convinced that I wanted the true tokens of a truly godly man, and also because by them I was convinced of the happy and blessed condition of him that was such a one.[6]

"Sharing our stories" is no recent discovery by Christians. Bunyan—and these women before him—had been doing that as a part of their evangelism for centuries. These women, living their normal Christian lives, talking with each other, were part of God's evangelistic plan. It wasn't only sermons that God used to convert John Bunyan; he used normal Christians.

Let me share one more story of God using ordinary Christians to spread the good news: the story of James Smith. Smith was a slave near Richmond, Virginia. He was also a Christian. The inhuman cruelty of his "masters" separated him from his family—his wife, Fanny, and their children—for decades. But Smith's Christian faith sustained him. Each night after his day's work, Smith preached the gospel of Jesus Christ to fellow slaves, even after his master whipped him for it. But it wasn't in Smith's capacity as a preacher that God gave him one of his most amazing opportunities to evangelize. Smith was sold to a plantation in Georgia. His new "owner," concerned about a lack of obedience in Smith, ordered his overseer to give Smith a beating to get Smith to obey instructions, particularly those designed to limit his praying and meeting with others to worship. The overseer lashed Smith's back one hundred times. One hundred times! Later, that same overseer overheard Smith praying for his—the overseer's—soul, and when he heard that, he was cut to the quick and begged Smith's forgiveness. He also encouraged him to escape.[7]

God calls all Christians to share the good news. Our churches need to make sure that we know the good news and to make sure that we can all express it clearly. And we should work to train each other in having the kind of Christian lives and clear understanding that will help us to share the gospel. If we are honest, the main reason that we often want to shift the responsibility for evangelism to others is that we are not exactly sure how to do it. That's the question we want to consider in our next chapter.

4

How Should We Evangelize?

How should we evangelize?

We evangelize by preaching the Word and spreading the message (see Rom. 10:17). Okay, but how particularly should we spread the Word? This is a more important question than some people have realized. Whatever the specific means may be, publicly through various media, privately by personal conversation, through print and sermons, or through conversation and group study—*how* should we spread the gospel?

I want us to consider this in a couple of ways. First, and most basically, there is a certain balance that we want to strive for in our evangelism, a balance of honesty and urgency and joy. Too often we have only one, or at best, two, of these aspects rather than all three. The balance is important. These three together most appropriately represent the gospel. And then secondly, in the second half of the chapter, I have some suggestions for specifically how we can spread the gospel.

The Balance

Honesty. First, we tell people with honesty that if they repent and believe, they will be saved. But they will need to repent, and it will be costly. We must be accurate in what we say, not holding any important parts back that seem to us awkward or off-putting.

When considering how to evangelize, many people don't like to include anything negative in their presentation. There are thought to be negative and positive approaches to sharing the gospel, and talking about sin and guilt and repentance and sacrifice is thought to be a negative one, which is why it is currently out of favor. Here's what one leading television preacher said: "I don't think that anything has been done in the name of Christ and under the banner of Christianity that has proven more destructive to human personality, and hence counterproductive to the evangelistic enterprise, than the unchristian, uncouth strategy of attempting to make people aware of their lost and sinful condition."[1] Others more theologically orthodox suggest that while judgment and guilt were culturally relevant to a previous generation, they are alien today. They suggest that people today will respond better to a message of freedom.

But according to the Bible, although freedom is a wonderful aspect of our message (e.g., John 8:32–36), sin and guilt are at the very heart and core of the gospel. Making people aware of their lost and sinful condition is part and parcel of sharing the good news of Christ. If you read the summaries of Peter's sermons in the early chapters of the book of Acts, you will see that Peter is breathtakingly honest about the sin of those to whom he's speaking. His remarks were not calibrated to be flattering. By being frank, Peter was faithfully following the method Jesus had used with Peter and the others just a few months before, saying, "Anyone who does not carry his cross and follow me cannot be my disciple" (Luke 14:27).

Think about it. Let's not believe that we are simply all engaged in some search for truth. The fall did not leave people neutral toward God but at enmity with him. Therefore we must not pretend that non-Christians are seekers by the simple virtue of their having been made in the image of God. The

Bible teaches that people are by nature estranged from God, and we must be honest about that.

What is repentance? It is turning from the sins you love to the holy God you're called to love. It is admitting that you're not God. It is beginning to value Jesus more than your immediate pleasure. It is giving up those things the Bible calls sin and leaving them to follow Jesus.

When we tell the gospel to people, we need to do it with honesty. To hold back important and unpalatable parts of the truth is to begin to manipulate and to try to sell a false bill of goods to the person with whom we are sharing. So however we evangelize, we aren't to hide problems, to ignore our own shortcomings, or to deny difficulties. And we are not to put forward only positives that we imagine our non-Christian friends presently value and present God as simply the means by which they can meet or achieve their own ends. We must be honest.

Urgency. Also, though, if we are to follow a biblical model of evangelism, we must emphasize the urgency with which people ought to repent and believe if they will be saved. They must decide now. They certainly shouldn't wait until a "better deal" comes along. People might be careful enough with their money to wait to sign up for a cell phone plan or to renew their current plan until they've looked around on the Internet, maybe phoning and getting two or three offers and then comparing them all. But there's no point here in waiting for a better offer for forgiveness. According to the New Testament (John 14:6; Acts 4:12; Romans 10; all of Hebrews), Christ is the only way. How else would we suggest that sinners and the holy God be reconciled? And if Christ is the only way, then what are we waiting for? We don't know that tomorrow is ours, and we shouldn't act as if it is (James 4:13). "Today, if you hear his voice, do not harden your hearts" (Ps. 95:7–8; Heb. 4:7).

Jesus once told this story:

> A man had a fig tree, planted in his vineyard, and he went to look for fruit on it, but didn't find any. So, he said to the man who took care of the vineyard for him, "For three years now I've been coming to look for fruit on this fig tree and haven't found any. Cut it down! Why should it use up the soil?"
>
> "Sir," the man replied, "leave it alone for one more year, and I'll dig around it and fertilize it. If it bears fruit next year, fine! If not, then cut it down." (Luke 13:6–9)

It's not manipulative or insensitive to bring up the urgent nature of salvation. It's simply the truth. The time of opportunity will end.

As Christians, we've come alive to the truth that history isn't cyclical, always repeating in an endless rotation of events, spinning till any given part of it becomes meaningless. No! We know that God has created this world, and that he will bring it to a close at the judgment. We know that he gives us life, and he takes it away. The time that we have is limited; the amount is uncertain, but the use of it is up to us. So Paul tells us in Ephesians to "make the most of every opportunity (5:16)."

Like a collector buying up a collection, we should desire to capture each fleeting hour and to turn it into a trophy for God and his grace. As Paul said, "The time is short. From now on . . . those who use the things of the world [should use them] as if not engrossed in them. For this world in its present form is passing away" (1 Cor. 7:29, 31).

What are your circumstances right now? Trust the Lord to use you in them instead of seeking for new ones. Don't let the passing permanence of your world or the lulling tedium of certain long hours and minutes make a fool of you. The days are "evil" (Eph. 5:16) in the sense that they are dangerous and fleeting, and we must redeem the time and make the most of every hour. So we say with Paul that, in view of a certain judgment, Christ's love compels us to tell the good news to others (see 2 Cor. 5:10–15). We must be honest not only about the cost of repentance, but also about the expiration date of the offer. Such honesty compels us to urgency.

Joy. Now, if I stopped here, we might wind up with some rather grim evangelists. Driven by a careful conscience to be clear about what is condemned and forbidden, and driven by a sense of the brevity of time, we could end up with an intense, forceful practice of evangelism. But this wouldn't seem so much like *good* news. It would be imbalanced and inaccurate, because Scripture uses so much love language in relation to the gospel. We are built to love love. God loves us. We love God. Christ has loved us, and we love him even though we have not seen him. This news is good exactly because we want to spend an eternity with him. An eternity in relative prosperity without him would actually be hell to us.

The truth of this news of a restored relationship with God brings us great joy. So we should joyfully tell people that if they repent and believe they will be saved. It is all worth it, despite the cost. Which one of the people recounted in Hebrews 11 would not say that it was worth it? The Lord Jesus himself endured the cross, we read, "for the joy set before him" (Heb. 12:2).

At our church in Washington we have a bronze plaque on the pillar at the entrance to the church parking lot with this saying of Jim Elliot's: "He is no fool who gives what he cannot keep to gain what he cannot lose." What do we gain in coming to Christ? We gain a relationship with God himself, which includes forgiveness, meaning, purpose, freedom, community, certainty, and hope. All these and so much more are found in Christ. Just because we are honest about the difficulties, we don't have to mask the blessings or deny God's specific goodnesses to us through the gospel. We don't have to make the demands of the gospel sound worse than they are simply to make it all sound credible. We should tell others the good news with joy.

So that's the balance that we want to see—honesty, urgency, and joy. Honesty and urgency with no joy gives us a grim determination (read Philippians). Honesty and joy with no urgency gives us a carelessness about time (read 2 Peter). And urgency and joy with no honesty leads us into distorted claims about immediate benefits of the gospel (read 1 Peter).

Having gotten that balance in mind, though, here are some more specific ideas of how we want to share the gospel.

Specific Suggestions

1) Pray. Remember the importance of prayer in your evangelism. When Jonah was saved from the fish, he said, "Salvation comes from the LORD" (Jonah 2:9). If the Bible teaches us that salvation is the work of God, then surely we should ask him to work among those we evangelize. Jesus did. His prayer in John 17 was for those who would believe in him through the disciples' preaching and witnessing. And God answered that prayer. Jesus said, "No one can come to me unless the Father who sent me draws him" (John 6:44). If this is God's work, we should ask him to do it.

Paul also prayed for the salvation of those he was witnessing to. He wrote to the Roman Christians, "Brothers, my heart's desire and prayer to God for the Israelites is that they may be saved" (Rom. 10:1). We can work and witness for the salvation of someone, but only God can finally bring it about. It is his work.[2] So we must pray.

I remember once sitting in the library at seminary in the midst of my studies when suddenly I was struck with the fact that several people I loved had not been converted, even though I had been praying for them regularly for years. For a few moments, I wondered what use all these studies were if God wasn't listening and answering prayers that would obviously glorify him. I struggled with discouragement about this. Nevertheless, I knew it was my duty to keep on praying.

Some of those people I was praying for have never, to my knowledge, been saved. But others have been saved. By God's grace, slowly but surely over the years, I have seen many people for whom I was praying more than twenty years ago come to know Christ. Humanly speaking, some of these conversions were unlikely and surprising, which shows that ultimately it is God who is at work in evangelism, not you or me alone. And that brings about some wonderful fruit.

We pray about much less significant matters every day. Why wouldn't we pray about this? When you evangelize, remember to pray.

2) Use the Bible. The Bible is not only for public preaching and private devotionals. It can also be used in evangelizing. An interesting example of this, one we noted earlier, is found in Acts 8, when Philip came to the Ethiopian official. The official was reading Isaiah 53, a famous prophecy about the Messiah. Philip, as it says in Acts 8:35, "began with that very passage of Scripture and told him the good news about Jesus." The Bible is God's Word and is inspired by God's Spirit. God's message can go out not just through your words and mine, but through his own inspired words. And we can know that he will take a special delight in showing the power of his Word as he uses it in conversions.

This is one reason that I so enjoy doing a study of Mark's Gospel as a tool of evangelism. I am confident that God will use his Word in ways that I wouldn't have known to plan. I remember my own conversion and how crucial in that was my reading through the Gospels. Introduce a non-Christian (or a whole group of them in a Bible study) to the person of Jesus Christ as he is revealed on the pages of Scripture. Let them interact with the primary sources. Watch the power and majesty and love and penetrating conviction of Christ come through the stories, the works, the teaching.

Referring to the clear teaching of the Bible also shows our friends that we are not simply giving them our own private ideas; rather, we are presenting Jesus Christ in his own life and teaching. Just as we want the preaching in our churches to be expositional—preaching in which the point of the message is the point of the Bible passage being preached—we want to see people exposed to God's Word because we believe that God desires to use his Word to bring about conversions. It is God's Word coming to us that his Spirit uses to reshape our lives.

In your evangelism, use the Bible.

3) **Be clear.** When you share the gospel, think carefully about the language you use. One of the best conversations I can remember having about evangelism was with a secular Jewish friend of mine. I was to give talks soon on a college campus about evangelism, and I decided to ask my friend about evangelism. We'll call him Michael. (In fact, that was his name.) "So, Michael," I said, "have you ever been evangelized?"

"What's that?" he asked.

"You know," I said, "when someone who is a Christian starts talking to you about God and Jesus and asking if you're saved."

"Oh, that!" he said. "Yeah, I guess I have been."

Anyway, Michael and I got into a long and good conversation. Now, the truth is that I had evangelized Michael a number of times before, but he hadn't realized that's what I was doing. As we talked about it now, it became clear that he thought evangelism was something that someone did *to* him rather than a conversation in which he could engage.

I also realized that in my previous conversations with him I had taken the meaning of words for granted. "God," "prayer," "heaven," "good," "moral," "judge," and "sin" are all words that I realized I had not done a good job defining. If I had simply gone through a quick, persuasive sales presentation and gotten him to say "yes!" he would have been saying yes to much that he didn't understand. We need to be both engaging and clear when we present the gospel.

None of us ever has a complete understanding of the gospel, but we must have a clear idea of the basics of our message, and we must be clear in our expression of them. If there is a likely misunderstanding, we should address it. We should speak in such a way as to be understood. *Contextualization* is the big theological word for this.

So, for example, when we talk about justification (and we should), we should make sure to define it. Justification is being declared right with God. But because we sin, we are not right with God. So how can we be declared right? We can't, if God is truly good—unless, that is, we have someone act as a substitute for us. *Justification*, then, gets us talking about all kinds of issues right at the heart of the gospel.

So, when we are talking to non-Christian friends about the gospel, we want to make sure they understand what we mean. Christians in the Bible had a great concern about this. So it's often been noted that Paul began with the Old Testament when he was speaking to Jews, but when he spoke to a group of Greeks in Athens (Acts 17) he began by quoting their own sayings. As he wrote to the Corinthians, "To the Jews I became like a Jew, to win the Jews. . . . To those not having the law I became like one not having the law . . . so as to win those not having the law" (1 Cor. 9:20–21).

One part of providing clarity when we share the gospel, sometimes missed by earnest evangelists, is the willingness to offend. Clarity with the claims of Christ certainly will include the translation of the gospel into words that our hearer *understands*, but it doesn't necessarily mean translating it into words that our hearer will *like*. Too often, advocates of relevant evangelism verge over into being advocates of irrelevant nonevangelism. A gospel that in no way offends the sinner has not been understood.

Look at Peter at Pentecost in Acts 2. Peter wanted to be relevant, but that relevance gave his words more bite, not less. How did Peter witness to those he wished to see saved? He said to them, among other things, "Let all Israel be assured of this: God has made this Jesus, whom you crucified, both Lord and Christ" (Acts 2:36).

Relevant? Yes. Pleasing? No. Clear? Undoubtedly.

We must be clear about the fact of sin (Isa. 59:1–2; Hab. 1:13; Rom. 3:22–23; 6:23; Eph. 2:8–9; Titus 3:5; 1 John 1:5–6). We must be clear about the meaning of the cross (Matt. 26:28; Gal. 3:10–13; 1 Tim. 1:15; 1 Pet. 2:24; 3:18). We must be clear about our need to repent of our sins and to trust in Christ (Matt. 11:28–30; Mark 1:15; 8:34; John 1:12; 3:16; 6:37; Acts 20:21). How can we really evangelize without being clear about what the Bible says about these issues?

4) Provoke self-reflection. Something typical of our age is a heightened defensiveness that leads people to discover things for themselves rather than hearing things from other people. The desire for original discovery is what's behind the "journey" language that some use today. "Let people find the truth themselves. The days of simple tracts and surefire, sales-presentation evangelism is over. Don't tell people something; talk with them. Have a conversation." That's what we are hearing we have to do today, and to that I have a couple of replies.

First, it's true. Second (and surprising to some) it's always been true. It's nothing new. Our parents and grandparents were not the naïve, unquestioning followers that so much of current literature makes them out to be. Skepticism about particular facts can be borne out of a general cynicism about truth or out of a deep certainty about human character. Sherlock Holmes asked questions not because he wanted to know someone else's perspective, *their* truth; he wanted to know *the* truth. Detective stories always presuppose a right and wrong with certain actions and motives that explain them. Otherwise, there's no puzzle to be solved.

We Christians know that there is a right and wrong, but we also know our own hearts. We know that we don't like to be shown up easily and clearly when we are in the wrong. I'm a pastor. I write books telling you what to do, and yet the other day my wife most lovingly and respectfully corrected me on something that I had said in the presence of our son. She was right. I was wrong. I believe in absolute truth. I know she loves me. I know the theological truth that I am sinful. And yet she had to labor with me with patience, determination, perseverance, and love to get me to even be in the position to consider that I was perhaps wrong in that situation. And I've been a Christian for over twenty years.

Defensiveness is natural to the fallen human heart, so we want to do our best to help people hear the good news. We want to live and talk in such a way that we provoke people to reflect on themselves, on their own desires and actions. We can do this by asking good questions—questions about the origin of life or about how they understand bad things in this world. We can ask about what they're struggling with in their lives, and what they think the answer might be. We can even ask them what they think about death, and Jesus, and God, and judgment, and the Bible, and Christianity. But afterward we'll have to do what some witnessing Christians find very hard to do, something that surprises some of our non-Christian friends—listen to their answers![3]

Ask good questions and listen to their answers. Explore them. You may be helping them to enunciate and articulate their own thinking for the first time ever. And you don't even need to try to pretend that this is easy for you.

This is what you do for someone you love, and you surely love the person you're witnessing to. Insofar as you have opportunity, befriend people. Lower their defensiveness toward you (but not toward your message). Make suggestions of what you think is the case. Be clear in your presentation of the gospel. Pray that you will be able to put things in such a way as to undermine their disbelief and cause them to doubt their denials of the truth of the gospel. Be provocative in your conversation.

In fact, try to live in a distinctly Christian "salty" way around them—in your words and actions. Make them thirsty. Make your whole life before them provocative. I sometimes introduce myself to people as being a fundamentalist, because I'm hoping there will be an intriguing disconnect between their assumptions of what a fundamentalist is and what kind of person I seem to be. Live a Christian life before them. And that brings me to my final suggestion for you.

5) **Use the church.** By "use the church," I mean invite the person to whom you're witnessing to the church at which you're a member or to some other gospel-preaching church. But by saying "use the church," I also mean so much more than that. Realize that how the Christian life is lived out in the Christian community is a central part of our evangelism. Like those washer-women that Bunyan overheard, our lives are to give our words credibility. Not that any of us can live perfectly, but we can live lives that commend the gospel. Remember

Jesus' words in the Sermon on the Mount: "Let your light shine before men, that they may see your good deeds and praise your Father in heaven" (Matt. 5:16; cf. 1 Pet. 2:12).

Remember Jesus' statement in John 13:34–35: "A new command I give you: Love one another. As I have loved you, so you must love one another. By this all men will know that you are my disciples, if you love one another." Our words alone are not a sufficient witness—we must speak; we have *news*. Our lives are the confirming echo of our witness. Evangelism should include our way of living and our way of living together in the new society that is the local church.

The temple in Jerusalem was destroyed in A.D. 70, and there is nothing about a great Christian temple in the New Testament—a place of grandeur and majesty to which we can point our non-Christian friends and say, "Look! Aren't you impressed? Doesn't this show how wonderful and mysterious and beautiful and true and good our God is?" What happened to the temple in the New Testament era? There is nothing like it, because the temple has become us. We Christians have together become the temple of the Holy Spirit. When you read the New Testament, you find that it's not our church buildings but us, Christians. We Christians have together become the temple of the Holy Spirit.

So the community we live in will be given hope by those of us who live distinctive Christian lives, not by your church or mine, not by how similar we are to those around us (a common mistake Christians can make), but by how attractively different we are. That's why we are to live the distinctive lives that we do—because we are God's picture, God's billboard, in our city. Thus Paul wrote to the Philippians, "Do everything without complaining or arguing, so that you may become blameless and pure, children of God, without fault in a crooked and depraved generation, in which you shine like stars in the universe as you hold out the word of life" (Phil. 2:14–16).

The people around us are lost in darkness; we have the wonderful and attractive call to live out a new life in our congregations—a good life that reflects the good news. Think about the role of your church in your evangelism. Yes, you can invite people to services and special evangelistic events, but also consider bringing them into your own life, into the network of relationships that is your congregation. That may be to them as a shining star in the dark night of their lives. That may provoke them to do some honest soul searching. They may ask, as a friend once asked me, "So, you're a Christian? Then tell me the gospel! Witness to me, or somethin'!"

Those are just some suggestions, but suggestions that I hope encourage you in evangelizing. Of course, sometimes we share the gospel wrongly because we misunderstand what evangelism actually is. And that brings us to our next question.

5

What *Isn't* Evangelism?

I remember as a little child hugging my father's leg at a gas station only to realize it wasn't his leg I was hugging. I was embarrassed! It was a case of mistaken identity.

Other times mistaken identity has more serious consequences. I'm amazed at the number of predatory animals that can camouflage their bodies so perfectly that their prey doesn't ever suspect that a branch or rock is actually another creature preparing to eat and run!

In the matter of evangelism, I'm concerned about a number of things that people take to be evangelism that aren't. And this case of mistaken identity can have consequences more serious than mere embarrassment. Let me mention five things mistaken for evangelism.

1) Imposition

Probably the most common objection to evangelism today is, "Isn't it wrong to impose our beliefs on others?"

Some people don't practice evangelism because they feel they are imposing on others. And the way evangelism is often done, I can understand the confusion! But when you understand what the Bible presents as evangelism, it's really not a matter of imposing your beliefs.

It's important to understand that the message you are sharing is not merely an opinion but a fact. That's why sharing the gospel can't be called an imposition, any more than a pilot can impose his belief on all his passengers that the runway is here and not there.

Additionally, the truths of the gospel are not yours, in the sense that they uniquely pertain to *you* or *your* perspective or experience, or in the sense that you came up with them. When you evangelize, you are not merely saying, "This is how I like to think of God," or "This is how I see it." You're presenting the *Christian* gospel. You didn't invent it, and you have no authority to alter it.

In biblical evangelism, we don't impose anything. In fact, we really can't. According to the Bible, evangelism is simply telling the good news. It's not making sure that the other person responds to it correctly. I wish we could, but according to the Bible, this is not something we can do. According to the Bible, the fruit from evangelism comes from God. As Paul wrote to the Corinthians:

> What, after all, is Apollos? And what is Paul? Only servants, through whom you came to believe—as the Lord has assigned to each his task. I planted the seed, Apollos watered it, but God made it grow. So neither he who plants nor he who waters is anything, but only God, who makes things grow. (1 Cor. 3:5–7; cf. 2 Cor. 3:5–6)

I remember one time in Cambridge talking with Bilal, a Lebanese Muslim friend of mine. We were talking about a mutual friend of ours who was a fairly secular Muslim. Bilal wanted our friend to embrace a more faithful Muslim lifestyle, and I wanted him to become a Christian. We commiserated together on the difficulty of living in the midst of a secular British culture. Bilal then commented on how corrupt the Christian country of Great Britain is. I responded that Britain is not a Christian country, that in fact there is no such thing as a Christian country. That, he said, quickly seizing the opportunity, is the problem with Christianity compared to Islam. Christianity, he said, does not provide answers and guidelines for all of the complexities of real life. It has no overarching social-political pattern to give to society. I responded that this is because of Christianity's realistic portrayal of the human condition, of the problem of the human situation. He asked me what I meant.

I said that Islam has a shallow understanding of man's problems because it teaches that our problems are basically a matter of behavior. The solution to our problem is merely a question of the will. However, Christianity, I said, has a much deeper, more accurate understanding of the human situation, which includes a frank admission of human sinfulness as not merely an aggregate of bad actions but as an expression of a bad heart in rebellion against God. It's a matter of human nature. I said that Christianity has nothing that Bilal would recognize as a comprehensive political program because we don't think that our real problem can be dealt with by political power. I could put a sword to a person's throat and make him a sufficiently good Muslim, but, I said, I can't make anyone a Christian that way.

The Bible presents the human problem as one that can never be solved by coercive force or imposition. Therefore, all I can do is present the good news accurately, live a life of love toward unbelievers, and pray for God to convict them of their sins and give them the gifts of repentance and faith.

True biblical, Christian evangelism by its very nature involves no coercion but only proclamation and love. We are to present the free gospel to all; we cannot manipulate anyone to accept it. Biblical Christians know that we can't coerce anyone into life.

2) Personal Testimony

Some think of personal testimony as evangelism. Surely personal testimony is a wonderful thing. The psalmist is a model of it: "Come and listen, all you who fear God; let me tell you what he has done for me" (Ps. 66:16). So, too, we see in the New Testament that the lives of Christians test, prove, and confirm the claims of Christ. Paul wrote to the Corinthians, "In him you have been enriched in every way—in all your speaking and in all your knowledge—because our testimony about Christ was confirmed in you" (1 Cor. 1:5–6). The truth of the gospel, which someone once shared with us, is proved in our lives daily. We should testify to this wonderful experience. We should delight in God and share our delight verbally with others. Such testimony can certainly *contribute* to evangelism.

Michael Green tells the story of being at an outreach event. It was a time that was full of Christians giving testimonies about their Christian life. At one point, Green recounted, a non-Christian professor leaned over to him and whispered: "You know, I don't believe any of this." Green responded, "Yeah, I know, but wouldn't you like to?" As recounted, "with that remark, tears welled up in the woman's eyes. Her head told her 'no,' but her heart yearned to hear."[1] Testimonies are powerful.

One of the classic testimonies was given by a blind man Jesus healed. When he was questioned after Jesus healed him, he responded, "Whether he [Jesus] is a sinner or not, I don't know. One thing I do know. I was blind but now I see!" (John 9:25). The man disregarded the menacing threats of those more honored and respected than he in order to give this verbal witness to the power of God. It's a wonderful, powerful testimony, but it's not evangelism. There is no gospel in it. The man didn't even know who Jesus was.

In our own congregation in Washington, one of the highlights of our morning service comes after the sermon on Sundays when we have baptisms. After a hymn is sung, the congregation is seated, and those who are to be baptized come forward. We ask them one by one to introduce themselves and to share their testimonies. We noticed, however, the first few times we did this, that people could recount their own conversions—and quite movingly—but without ever clearly sharing the gospel. While it was encouraging for the congregation gathered there, the non-Christians present (including friends and families of those to be baptized) weren't hearing the gospel in the testimonies.

So we began asking those coming forward for baptism to write out their testimony the week before and to go over it with a staff member. One of the main things such a check does is to make sure that the gospel isn't merely implicit in the testimony but is, rather, explicit and clear, so that non-Christians present will be evangelized even as they're listening to the testimony of their friend. An account of a changed life is wonderful and inspiring thing, but it's the gospel of Jesus Christ that explains what it's all about and how it happened. And it's the gospel that turns sharing a testimony into evangelism.

Certainly a testimony of what we know God to have done in our lives may include the good news, but it also may not. In telling people how we have seen God help us, we may not actually make clear his claim on our lives or explain what Christ did on the cross. It's good to share a testimony of what God has done in our lives, but in sharing our testimonies we may not actually make clear what Christ's claims are on other people. In order to evangelize, we must be clear about that.

Let me share with you one word of special caution. Testimony is, of course, popular in our postmodern, that's-good-for-you age. Who would object to your thinking you've gotten something good from Christ? But wait and see what happens when you try to move the conversation from what Jesus has done for you to the facts of the life, death, and resurrection of Christ, and how that all applies to your nonbelieving friend. That's when you discover that testimony is not necessarily evangelism.

3) Social Action and Public Involvement

Some people mistake social action and public involvement for evangelism.

As this book is being written, a new biography of William Jennings Bryan has just been released. Bryan was the Democratic candidate for president of the United States three times. He was a fervent evangelical Christian, an evangelist in his own right, and a tireless worker for social reforms. He went all over the country giving speeches on factory conditions, working for a shorter workweek, promoting the idea of minimum wages, and championing graduated taxation. While Bryan was so laboring, was he evangelizing? Certainly he was involved with the best of motivations for the good of the most vulnerable members of society. His desire to change societal wrongs was excellent; his desires commend the character of the God Bryan claimed to represent. But was he evangelizing?

If someone had agreed that Bryan was pointing out real problems but disagreed with the solution he offered, would that have indicated he was also opposed to evangelism, the gospel, and the kingdom of God? I remember one prominent evangelical leader in the 1980s who was a proponent of unilateral nuclear disarmament. He upheld the idea that regardless of what "the other side" did, the United States government should simply eliminate their nuclear weapons. He justified this in the name of advocating peace. But what if such action, ironically, despite all the best intentions, actually encouraged war? Or what if peace was actually best achieved by "peace through nuclear superiority," as one t-shirt said?

Of the many actions designed to improve society, some are wonderful (e.g., the abolition of slavery), and some are terrible (e.g., legalizing the killing of unborn children). But none of them, not even the best, are the gospel of Jesus Christ.

Being involved in mercy ministries may help to *commend* the gospel, which is why Jesus taught, "Let your light shine before men, that they may see your good deeds and praise your Father in heaven" (Matt. 5:16). Peter echoed this when he wrote that we should "live such good lives among the pagans that, though they accuse you of doing wrong, they may see your good deeds and glorify God on the day he visits us" (1 Pet. 2:12). Displaying God's compassion and kindness by our actions is a good and appropriate thing for Christians to do. Jesus commended it when he told the story of the sheep and the goats (Matthew 25). Matthew concluded that story by quoting the Lord: "Whatever you did not do for one of the least of these, you did not do for me" (Matt. 25:45). But such actions are not evangelism. They commend the gospel, but they share it with no one. To be *evangelism*, the gospel must be clearly communicated, whether in written or oral form.

When our eyes fall from God to humanity, social ills replace sin, horizontal problems replace the fundamental vertical problem between us and God, winning elections eclipses winning souls. But Proverbs 11:30 says, "The fruit of the righteous is a tree of life, and he who wins souls is wise." Our practice of evangelism might be crusades for public virtues, or for programs of compassion, or for other social changes. But, as Donald McGavran, the well-known missionary from the middle of the last century, said, "Evangelism is not proclaiming the desirability of a liquorless world and persuading people to vote for prohibition. Evangelism is not proclaiming the desirability of sharing the wealth and persuading people to take political action to achieve it."[2]

Evangelism is not declaring God's political plan for nations nor recruiting for the church—it is a declaration of the gospel to individual men and women. Societies are challenged and changed when, through this gospel, the Lord brings individual men and women together in churches to display his character and to pursue their own callings in the world. As we learn from King David, it is a good thing to govern well (see 2 Sam. 23:3–4), but it is not evangelism. It's also a good thing to be a husband, wife, father, mother, employer, or employee—the list could go on. These are parts of what Christians are called to do, but fulfilling them is not the same thing as obeying the command to share the gospel of Jesus Christ.

4) Apologetics

Other people mistake apologetics for evangelism. Like the activities we've considered above, apologetics itself is a good thing. We are instructed by Peter to be ready to give a reason for the hope that we have (1 Pet. 3:15). And apologetics is doing exactly that. Apologetics is answering questions and objections people may have about God or Christ, or about the Bible or the message of the gospel.

Apologists for Christianity argue for its truth. They maintain that Christianity better explains that sense of longing that all people seem to have. Christianity better explains human rationality. It fits better with order. They may argue (as C. S. Lewis does in *Mere Christianity*) that it better fits with the moral sense that people innately have. It copes better with problems of alienation and anxiety. Christians may—and should—argue that Christianity's frankness about death and mortality commends it. These can be good arguments to have.

Other times they're not. Once, when I was giving a series of evangelistic talks at a university in England, I was so taken up in one talk with trying to anticipate objections to the Christian gospel—and answer them!—that I fear I suggested new ways to doubt the gospel far more effectively than I presented it to anyone that night. Since I used to be an agnostic, apologetics have been very important to me. God used things such as reasoning about the resurrection of Christ to help bring me to faith in Christ. But not all people have the same questions. We are not all built the same. And I shouldn't evangelize in such a way that I'm assuming that every non-Christian is just like I was with all my issues, questions, objections, and arguments.

However, just as we've observed with giving a testimony or working for social justice, practicing apologetics is a good thing, but it's not evangelism. Answering questions and defending parts of the good news may often be a part of conversations Christians have with non-Christians, and while that may have been a part of our own reading or thinking or talking as we came to Christ, such activity is not evangelism.

Apologetics can present wonderful opportunities for evangelism. Being willing to engage in conversations about where we came from or what's wrong with this world can be a significant way to introduce honest discussions about the gospel. For that matter, Christians can raise questions with their non-Christian friends about the purpose of life, what will happen after death, or the identity of Jesus Christ. Any of these topics will take work and careful thought, but they can easily lead into evangelism.

In college I led a discussion group for many of my college friends who were atheists. We met in a dorm room, just a number of atheists and me and occasionally another Christian. The atheists set the agenda. They posed questions, and we discussed them. I would try to answer their questions, and I'd also ask them some of my own. At the end of the day, for all the time it took, I can't really say how helpful that meeting was.

It should also be said that apologetics has its own set of dangers. You might unwittingly confirm someone in their unbelief by your inability to answer questions that are impossible to answer anyway. You can easily leave the impression that if you don't know how to answer your friends' questions, then you don't really know enough to believe that the Christian gospel is true either. But just because we don't know everything doesn't mean we don't know anything. All knowledge in this world is limited. We proceed from what we know, and we work that out. Everyone, from the youngest child to the most celebrated research scientist, does this. Apologetics can be very important work, but it should be undertaken with care.

By far the greatest danger in apologetics is being distracted from the main message. Evangelism is not defending the virgin birth or defending the historicity of the resurrection. Apologetics is defending the faith, answering the questions others have about Christianity. It is responding to the agenda that others set. Evangelism, however, is following Christ's agenda, the news about him. Evangelism is the positive act of telling the good news about Jesus Christ and the way of salvation through him.

5) The Results of Evangelism

Finally, one of the most common and dangerous mistakes in evangelism is to misinterpret the *results* of evangelism—the conversion of unbelievers—for evangelism itself, which is the simple telling of the gospel message. This may be the most subtle misunderstanding, yet it is a misunderstanding still. Evangelism must not be confused with its fruit. Now, if you combine this misunderstanding with a misunderstanding of the gospel itself, and of what the Bible teaches about conversion, then it is very possible to end up thinking not only that evangelism is seeing others converted, but thinking that it is within our power to do it!

According to the Bible, converting people is not in our power. And evangelism may not be defined in terms of results but only in terms of faithfulness to the message preached. John Stott has said, "To 'evangelize' . . . does not mean to win converts . . . but simply to announce the good news, irrespective of the results."[3] At the Lausanne gathering in 1974, evangelism was defined as follows:

> To evangelize is to spread the good news that Jesus Christ died for our sins and was raised from the dead according to the Scriptures, and that as the reigning Lord he now offers the forgiveness of sins and the liberating gift of the Spirit to all who repent and believe.[4]

Paul wrote, "We are to God the aroma of Christ among those who are being saved and those who are perishing. To the one we are the smell of death; to the other, the fragrance of life. And who is equal to such a task?" (2 Cor. 2:15–16). Note that the same ministry has two different effects. As with the parable of the soils, it's not that certain evangelistic techniques always lead to conversions. The same seed was planted in various places. The response varied not according to how the seed was planted but according to the nature of the soil. Just as Paul could not judge whether he was preaching correctly based upon how people responded to his message, so we cannot finally judge the correctness of what we do by the immediate response that we see.

Making this error distorts well-meaning churches into pragmatic, results-oriented businesses. It also cripples individual Christians with a sense of failure, aversion, and guilt. As one book puts it:

> Evangelism is not persuading people to make a decision; it is not proving that God exists, or making out a good case for the truth of Christianity; it is not inviting someone to a meeting; it is not exposing the contemporary dilemma, or arousing interest in Christianity; it is not wearing a badge saying 'Jesus Saves'! Some of these things may be right and good in their place, but none of them should be confused with evangelism. To evangelize is to declare on the authority of God what he has done to save sinners, to warn men of their lost condition, to direct them to repent, and to believe in the Lord Jesus Christ.[5]

Who can deny that much modern evangelism has become emotionally manipulative, seeking simply to cause a momentary decision of the sinner's will, yet neglecting the biblical idea that conversion is the result of the supernatural, gracious act of God toward the sinner?

D. Martyn Lloyd-Jones recalls the story of a man who was disappointed that Lloyd-Jones hadn't given a public altar call after the previous night's sermon. "'You know, doctor, if you had asked me to stay behind last night I would have done so.'

"'Well,' I said, 'I am asking you now, come with me now.'

"'Oh no,' he replied, 'but if you had asked me last night I would have done so.'

"'My dear friend,' I said, 'if what happened to you last night does not last for twenty-four hours I am not interested in it. If you are not as ready to come with me now as you were last night you have not got the right, the true thing. Whatever affected you last night was only temporary and passing, you still do not see your real need of Christ.'"[6]

And such problems sometimes go further by becoming established in a church culture. One minister recounted:

> I sat across the table from a 'big' preacher. His church had five thousand on a Sunday morning. I asked him about his evangelism strategy. He said his church employed

two seminary students, each of whom was required to have two people come forward for baptism each Sunday. Therefore, a minimum of four people would 'profess faith' each Sunday—208 a year. He added, 'You can't get invitations to evangelism conferences unless you baptize 200 a year.' I was dumbfounded! I probed a bit. 'What if Sunday comes and the seminarian doesn't have two who will profess faith?' He responded, 'I will get students who can get the job done.' I questioned, 'What if these fellows are forced to cut some theological corners to meet their quota?' He was unconcerned and thought my question trivial, pesky, and the child of a too lively conscience.[7]

When we are involved in a program in which converts are quickly counted, decisions are more likely pressed, and evangelism is gauged by its immediately obvious effect, we are involved in undermining real evangelism and real churches. History is full of people coming to Christ months and years after the gospel is presented to them. That may be the case with you. I know it was with me, and it is with many other Christians. Most of us don't respond the first time we hear the gospel. Do you know the story of Luke Short?

It took a long time for the conversion of Mr. Short. He was a New England farmer who lived to be one hundred years old. Sometime in the middle of the 1700s he was sitting in his fields reflecting on his long life. As he did, "he recalled a sermon he had heard in Dartmouth [England] as a boy before he sailed to America. The horror of dying under the curse of God was impressed upon him as he meditated on the words he had heard so long ago and he was converted to Christ—eighty-five years after hearing John Flavel preach."[8] The preacher, John Flavel, had been a faithful evangelist eighty-five years earlier. And he was wiser than to have thought that the day he preached the sermon, he would quickly see all its fruit.

The Christian call to evangelism is a call not simply to

persuade people to make decisions but rather to proclaim to them the good news of salvation in Christ, to call them to repentance, and to give God the glory for regeneration and conversion. We don't fail in our evangelism if we faithfully tell the gospel to someone who is not converted; we fail only if we don't faithfully tell the gospel at all. Evangelism itself isn't converting people; it's telling them that they need to be converted and telling them how they can be.

Evangelism is not an imposition of our ideas upon others. It is not merely personal testimony. It is not merely social action. It may not involve apologetics, and it is not the same thing as the results of evangelism. Evangelism is telling people the wonderful truth about God, the great news about Jesus Christ. When we understand this, then obedience to the call to evangelize can become certain and joyful. Understanding this increases evangelism as it moves from being a guilt-driven burden to a joyful privilege.

But what happens once we've understood correctly what evangelism is, and we've done it? What happens then? That's what we'll take up in our next chapter.

6

What Should We Do
After We Evangelize?

I had assured my young Christian friend that I would do all of the talking. "Besides," I said, "people are often interested in having a conversation. And even if they're not, most people are very polite."

I don't think my friend was buying it, but he followed along with me. When we came up to the first guy, reading a book, leaning with his back against a large, old tree, I began to engage him in conversation.

He just looked up at me, seeming mildly irritated, and said, "Go to hell!" While we didn't follow his instructions, we did move on at that point.

As my friend and I continued initiating conversations, we found different responses. And that's the way it is with all our evangelism. We get various responses to the gospel. This is true in contact evangelism. And this is true in the more long-term-relationship evangelism that we are doing all the time with our non-Christian friends.

When people are confronted with Jesus' command to repent and believe, many people do, and many people don't. And with those who do, their responses don't all look alike. Even those who reject the gospel don't all do it in the same way.

Negative Responses

"*I'm undecided.*" Most of us have trouble making up our minds from time to time. We might be very decisive about some matters but not at all about others. We want to delay many decisions as long as possible in order to leave our options open.

I was an "undecided" for years. I spent probably two to four years (depending on how I count) considering the claims of Christ. I understand now from John 3:36 that as long as I was unbelieving, God's wrath remained on me. But at the same time, I was reading the Bible and thinking about following Christ. From a theological standpoint, I would now say that God was drawing me. But at the time, the Christians around me could see only that I was an "undecided." And that's all I could see of myself.

Considered at one level, people are undecided for various reasons. Maybe they aren't sure of their need and, therefore, of the importance of the message we are sharing with them. They might be undecided on something as basic as the existence of God or whether we, the ones sharing the message, are confident about the truth of the Bible. A lot of people are undecided simply because they are apathetic and indifferent. They're not convinced that they're in any danger. They can't conceive of anything they might have done that would be bad enough to merit any kind of terrible consequences from which they need to be saved. But whatever the reason, they're not sure. They're not aware of the danger of indifference to God, let alone their rebellion against him personally. Being undecided, they might reason, is not the same as being against something or someone.

Of course, "undecideds" don't count—at least, not as disciples. Silence may be construed as consent in legal reasoning, but it isn't in following Jesus. Jesus said, "He who is not with me is against me" (Matt. 12:30; Luke 11:23).[1] If people tell us that they can't make up their mind, we can't force them to, but at the same time we must not comfort them in their indecision, as if God recognizes the validity of a kind of spiritual in-between state. In humanity's rebellion against God, there is no neutrality.

In the book of Acts, Luke records Paul's preaching to all kinds of people. Among them were people Paul evangelized who did not respond by repenting and believing, but who wanted to hear him again.

We know that Felix, the Roman governor of Caesarea, told Paul after Paul had witnessed to him, "That's enough for now! You may leave. When I find it convenient, I will send for you" (Acts 24:25). But when we continue to read, we find that Felix's motivation was greed. Felix "was hoping that Paul would offer him a bribe, so he sent for him frequently and talked with him" (Acts 24:26).

A little different was Paul's witnessing to King Agrippa. After Paul had shared the gospel with him, Agrippa responded, "Do you think that in such a short time you can persuade me to be a Christian?" (Acts 26:28). That was essentially a negative response. Agrippa was rebuffing Paul's evangelistic witness and even seeming to reprove him for his forwardness. It's interesting that Agrippa didn't simply deny the gospel, but rather he implied that, were he to become convinced of it, he would need more time to do so.

We can't know what Agrippa was thinking. And we may not know what those we've witnessed to are thinking. But they should know that, even if they don't think that they are making up their minds about Christ, they are still making up their lives. They can't help it. They will either live as if Christ is Lord or as if he's not. We can hold our conclusions in suspense; we can't hold our living in suspense. No one will ever experience a truce in the conflict of lordship. There are only two options. And each of us in the world lives as if only one of these is Lord—God or self.[2]

Another negative response is "*I want to wait.*" Not only was I an "undecided"; I was also a "wait." A "wait" is a lot like an "undecided." A "wait" may or may not be an "undecided"; both waiting and not deciding have some similarities. Those who are undecided do wait. But they may wait simply because they don't want the consequences of a decision. A "wait" could be a person who doesn't want to close the door on Christian faith by rejecting it, at least not yet. Or he could be a person who doesn't want to repent of his sins, at least not yet. Such people may not be self-consciously undecided, but they want freedom from having to make a decision. For whatever reason, they want more time.

As with the "undecided," we should respect the "wait." We can't force someone to make a decision. We can't force her to make up her mind. But we can be clear about the danger of waiting.

Waiting is a negative response, even if couched in the most polite, ambivalent hesitation. "Wait" is another form of "no." That doesn't mean that it can never become a yes, but it isn't one yet. Both "no" and "wait" can, by God's grace, be turned into a "yes" to the gospel but until that time, both are "no" answers.

A famous story about the danger of a delayed response involves the famous nineteenth-century evangelist D. L. Moody. As an evangelistic meeting he was holding came to a close, Moody said, "Now, I want you to take that question with you and think it over, and next Sunday I want you to come back and tell me what you are going to do with it." His song leader, Ira Sankey, sang a hymn, "Today the Savior Calls." Sometime after the meeting that night, a fire began.

And before noon the next day, much of Chicago had been destroyed by fire, including Moody's own church building. Perhaps as many as three hundred people were killed, and thousands were made homeless. Moody vowed, as a response to this, that he would never again give a congregation a week to think over their need for salvation.

If, after you have evangelized people, they give you a "I want to wait" response, they may be expressing fear of the demands that would come on them if they were to commit themselves. "Wait" means I want something to stay like it is right now.

If you sense that they are not really attracted to the gospel, be clear and then drop it. Continue to pray for them. Make sure they understand what you are saying, but realize that you have indeed evangelized. You have witnessed. You have shared the gospel. You have been faithful. We share, but, as Paul told the Corinthians, "I planted the seed, Apollos watered it, but God made it grow" (1 Cor. 3:6). Clearly, more has to happen inside these people, and we should aid by praying for the Spirit's work and by trying to live a salty, provocative, attractive, joyful, authentic life around our friends.

Perhaps they want to wait, because, although they have basically decided to continue as they are—apart from Christ—they want to preserve their relationship with you. They know you are a Christian. They want your approval, or at least your friendship. And so, rather than cutting you off, they simply avoid, procrastinate, and delay. They wait.

On the other hand, perhaps they recognize that they are becoming convinced, that they are deciding to follow Christ. But they are reluctant to repent of certain sins. Perhaps it's a relationship with a girlfriend, a love of getting drunk, or a desire to continue in a sinful avoidance of responsibility. Whatever it is, they find within themselves, as they're coming to recognize the truth of the gospel and to take seriously God's claim on their lives, a desire to pause. "Hold on!" they say. "Am I really sure I want to give up this much?" I can understand that reaction. While sin's ugliness is often apparent once we have given up a particular sin, it was once attractive, even beguiling, to us.

So, if you sense that someone is becoming attracted to the gospel, be patient. I've read books on personal evangelism that talk about the need to protect a person's privacy while they are deciding. I remember one book that even suggested we should lock the door so that we and the one we are leading to Christ won't be interrupted. I wonder about that . . .

I don't know what you think, but I agree with D. Martyn Lloyd-Jones's statement in the previous chapter to the man who wanted to make a decision one evening but did not because Lloyd-Jones hadn't given a public invitation. The man told him the next day that he wouldn't be making a decision at all, though he would have the previous night. Lloyd-Jones responded, "If what happened to you last night does not last for twenty-four hours I am not interested in it. If you are not as ready to come with me now as you were last night you have not got the right, the true thing. Whatever affected you last night was only temporary and passing, you still do not see your real need of Christ."[3]

Interrupting someone in the process of deciding to follow Christ can actually help him. After all, his life as a Christian will be full of interruptions, of people who will distract, disturb, discourage, and even mock him for following Christ. Having a little of that right at the beginning is no bad thing.

As I'm writing this section, I've been watching a squirrel in our backyard. At first he was perched on the fence and about to leap to a tree branch. But he waited. He stood there for several seconds, eyeing the branch, poised to spring, but not yet springing. He was waiting. I don't know why. I guess it was to make sure the moment was right, that the wind wasn't too high, or that our dogs weren't around, or that there was no other predator awaiting him in the tree. Who knows what all was involved in that situation? But the squirrel waited.

People can be like that too. Even if they've decided that they want to become a Christian, they realize that what we've described to them will mean a tremendous change. A new turn in their lives—a new life, really—is about to begin. I can understand the natural tendency to pause and take stock. To wait—even if for the squirrel's few moments—before they take the plunge. Pray for wisdom to know how to respond, even as you pray for God's Spirit to continue his work in their hearts.

Another negative answer is "*Not now.*" I won't say much about a "not now." Most of it has been covered in our consideration of an "undecided" and a "wait." A "not now" says, "I might think about it more later, but I'm not persuaded. I don't like the cost. I'm not just a 'wait.' I'm being a little more definitive. I'm saying, 'No—at least, for right now.' I'm not an 'undecided.' I understand that you want me to follow Christ now, and to that I'm saying no. Perhaps at some point in the future I might think differently about this, but for this year, this month, for today, as I see things, I'm saying, 'No. Not now.'"

I was a "not now." I wasn't sure that Christianity was wrong; I was an agnostic. And even when I began moving toward Christianity, as I read the Gospels, I pondered for quite a while, turning over the question of becoming a Christian and concluding, "Not now." I thought it was too much to take in all at once and commit to. But I continued to read, attend church, and think. I didn't really pray, at least, not much.

Of course, there are less hopeful "not now's." A "not

now" can be a decided "no" expressed with some humility. Or he might be expressing a realization that he's open to his mind being changed, even though it hasn't happened yet. It can also be a polite way of saying the next response we want to consider.

"*No, never.*" I don't think I was ever a "no, never." This is the most severely negative response. Paul implicitly said "no, never" in Acts 7 and 8 as he went around persecuting Christians, even approving of Stephen's martyrdom. A "no, never" is saying "I've looked at Christianity all it needs to be looked at, and I've considered it all it needs to be considered. The passage of time will not change anything about this. The message is simply not true. It's certainly not true for me!"

The certainty of the "no, never" obviously informs us of how strongly the person feels. However, it doesn't tell us with unfailing accuracy what will end up happening. I'm sure that many Christians—you may be one of them—were at one time "no, nevers."

According to the Bible, non-Christians are spiritually blind. Their eyes are not open to spiritual truths. They are dead to the things of God. Their own statements on spiritual things may be sincere, but they're not necessarily accurate.

Of course, those who adamantly reject the gospel must still be treated with respect. We don't need to make an appeal to them every time we see them. Such appeals may simply drive them away. To friends like this we should continue to be faithful, knowing that the very strength of their response may indicate a strength God will someday convert and use for his own ends. Paul was a mighty opponent of the gospel, and yet he became a mighty evangelist. As with other negative responses, this one, too, is best met with continued prayer, and we can continue to live around the "no, nevers" in such a way as to demonstrate the great truths of the Christian gospel. Let them see your life and character. We can let them see our church family, a community of Christians following Christ together, helping and caring for each other.

Positive Responses

Now let's think about those who accept the gospel.

What do you do with those people who accept the news you've given and profess repentance and faith? No one book can fully answer this question. Certainly not this one. The Bible, however, gives us all the instructions that we need. And we find there that these new Christians are to be brought into the fellowship of the local church. They're to be given all the family privileges and all the family responsibilities. They're to be baptized and admitted to the Lord's Table. They are to be provided with guidance and counsel, love and support, care and teaching. Their relationship with the local church will mature and change just like their relationships with their spouse or friends. Sometimes one thing is needed; at another stage of life other kinds of support, correction, or instruction will be needed.

Throughout it all, the new Christian should continue to be taught what it means to follow Jesus. From sitting under the preaching of the Word, to being baptized and taking the Lord's Supper, to praying and studying the Word, to repenting and believing, evangelism should find its fulfillment in discipleship. The good news is not merely about the commuting of an eternal sentence but about the commencing of an eternal relationship. Truly trusting Christ will always show itself by following him.

However, some "yeses" are false ones. Sometimes people say that they have become a Christian when they haven't. Some of these will no doubt be revealed to us only in the next world. Sometimes this becomes obvious after years of apparent discipleship. Other times it happens more quickly, after only a few weeks, months, or years of Christian profession. Their zeal seems to lag. Their church attendance becomes spotty. They would continue to say they are Christians, but following Christ is of little practical concern to them. Little of their energy goes into it, little of their attention.

And then one day the flickering flame just seems to go out. It is extinguished by the cares of this world, the lust of the flesh, the pride of life. Jesus told a parable about the plants that sprang up quickly but then quickly died (Mark 4:5–7). It's exactly because of such supposedly sincere but actually false conversions that Christians have often been exhorted to be patient in their offering of assurance and in their counting of converts. George Whitefield said, "There are so many stony ground hearers, who receive the Word with joy, that I have determined to suspend my judgment till I know the tree by its fruits. I cannot believe they are converts until I see fruit brought back; it will never do a sincere soul any harm."[4]

I remember talking to a friend with whom I'd been study-ing Mark's Gospel. He told me one morning—after months of meeting—that he'd become a Christian. I asked him some questions, rejoiced with him, took him over to meet with the church staff to share his great news with them. Afterward we all prayed with him, and then the staff members filed out of the room until my friend and I were left alone again. I closed the door, sat down, and said, "I'm not sure exactly what's really happened to you, but it sounds like God is doing great things in your life. Time will tell." (I said more, but that's all that I need to recount for the point I'm making!) And time did tell. As we approached his baptism, he was confronted with further sins. At each one of those points, he had the choice to continue to follow God and trust Christ or, as he came to understand more clearly what repentance meant for his life, of turning back and deciding to live for himself and for his immediate pleasure as his god.

Praise God, he chose to follow Christ! My friend and those like him are the true "yeses," which are the evangelist's hope. These are the true Christians. At one time, we were not Christians. Perhaps you were converted when you were a small child. You may not remember a time when you didn't follow Christ. But the Bible tells us that we are all by nature at enmity with God. And at some point, our hearts came alive to God and our wills bent to his. We were converted. That's what we want to see as a result of our evangelism.

But is getting this result what motivates us to evangelize? If a yes answer seems obvious to you, don't skip the next chapter. We'll see why we should really go to so much trouble to share the good news.

7

Why Should We Evangelize?

So, we've seen that God calls us to evangelize, and he tells us how to do it. The message is about him. But we have one final question to consider: Why should we evangelize? In other words, what's the ultimate goal?

The French philosopher and mathematician Blaise Pascal once said, "Happiness is the motive of every man, even those who hang themselves." Really? Is our own happiness the reason that we do everything that we do? Or are there other motives as well?

But why even ask the question? Is there such a thing as having the wrong motivation for evangelism? Now, maybe this seems to be a silly question. After all, how bad can it be to share the gospel? Won't any reason do? What's the point of looking for a motive for something that is, in and of itself, evidently good? Isn't that like looking for a motive to love your spouse or to care for your kids? What can be gained from such assessment?

But there are problems when the motive is wrong. For example, you could have a *selfish* motive for evangelism. As grotesque as it may seem, you could evangelize out of wanting to be right, or wanting to win an argument with a friend, or wanting some kind of psychological reenforcement for your own beliefs, or wanting to look spiritual in front of your friends—or even in front of God—or to have a reputation as a successful evangelist. I know that sometimes I've shared the gospel, at least in part, so that I could tell others that I had witnessed to someone. I'm not particularly proud of that fact, but it's true.

So what is the right reason to tell the good news?

According to the Bible, good motives for evangelism are a desire to be obedient, a love for the lost, and a love for God. Let's consider each one of these. And then I'll close this chapter with a few encouragements.

A Desire to Be Obedient

When we read the Bible, we see that evangelism isn't an idea thought up by traveling revivalists or marketing specialists. It was the risen Lord Jesus Christ who commanded his disciples to "go and make disciples of all nations, baptizing them in the name of the Father and of the Son and of the Holy Spirit" (Matt. 28:19). We know from the book of Acts that the early disciples did this. And Paul refers to his own compulsion to preach the gospel (1 Cor. 9:16–17). Preaching the gospel was an obligation he had been given (Rom. 1:14). To evangelize was to obey.

And the command wasn't only given to these original disciples. We considered this back in chapter 3, but here's a brief refresher. We read in Acts 8:4: "Those who had been scattered preached the word wherever they went," and those scattered ones weren't just apostles or elders. Later on in Acts 8 we find the story of Philip the deacon evangelizing the Ethiopian official.

One of the clearest places in the New Testament where we find the command to evangelize is 1 Peter. In chapter 3, Peter commands young Christians: "Be prepared to give an answer to everyone who asks you to give the reason for the hope that you have" (1 Pet. 3:15). Doing so is said to be a part of setting apart Christ as Lord, that is, of obeying him.

We know that God is good. And we know that if we fear him uniquely (as Peter urged Christians to do), it's as if we are tied to him, and we must go where he leads. Have you ever been (or even watched) waterskiing? Following Christ is a bit like that. The person on the skis has special regard and respect for one particular boat, because it is that boat which determines where the one on the skis will go. Sometimes the lake may be placid and the water calm. At such times the skier may have no particular problem following the boat. But sometimes the boat goes through some rougher water. Then, as long as the skier is holding on to the tow rope, the skier, too, will go through rough water.

God is much better than any boat driver at knowing where we need to go, but it is the universal experience of all of us who are Christians that God will take us through some difficult waters. However, if we are truly going to fear him alone, then we will continue following him, doing good, and evangelizing, even when doing so entails suffering.

"But," some of you may be thinking, "today differs so much from the days in which Peter wrote. Where then there was tormenting persecution, today there is only tolerant pluralism, at least for us in the West. What does such talk of being willing to suffer mean for us in our prosperity and spiritual indifference? This stuff about suffering doesn't really apply to us, does it?"

I think it does. Robert Jenson, in one essay, gave an example of what it could mean. He noted:

> One of [the] chief and excruciatingly ironic effects [of the ideology of pluralism]: it silences a lot of people. . . . So far as my observation reaches, the silenced are almost always those who if they spoke would say something character-

istically Jewish or Christian or Islamic. Try, for example, arguing that unrestricted permission to abort the unborn is a social and political evil at a party in Manhattan or a college town in Minnesota. Your arguments will not be rebutted; heads will merely be turned as from one who has audibly broken wind. If, on the other hand, you argue what is in fact the *conventional* opinion, you will be praised for courage and compassion. Or relate two conversions, one to Christianity and the other away from it; one will be received as a tale of horrid narrow-mindedness and the other as an example of an open society's marvelous possibilities.[1]

Have you ever tried to be open about your Christian discipleship? If so, you know that sometimes it's a wonderful experience, but other times you're simply made to feel strange or stupid.

We typically want to process our experiences immediately, and if they are unpleasant, we are inclined to change course in order to some way avoid the discomfort of the difficult comment or the pain that comes to us by a long obedience. But Peter says (1 Peter 3) that navigating our lives that way won't do; at least, not for those who really want to serve God more than themselves. Because this world is in rebellion against God and good, and if we would fear him and follow him, then our former false peace will leave, and we will become the focus of a pitched battle, sometimes around us, sometimes inside us. Following a good God in an evil world will sometimes involve suffering—even as we evangelize. But we do it, because we are believers in Jesus Christ.

If you are a believer, you have been commanded to share the good news of Jesus Christ with others.

Love for the Lost

Another reason to share the gospel is out of love for those who are lost. It is a godly, Christlike thing to have compassion and mercy on those in need. God himself, we read, "so loved the world that he gave his one and only Son, that whoever believes in him shall not perish but have eternal life" (John 3:16). If God has loved in this way, we, too, should love those who are lost. We ourselves have been the objects of his saving love, so how very appropriate it is for us to show such love to others. The Lord Jesus, whom we follow, "when he saw the crowds . . . had compassion on them, because they were harassed and helpless, like sheep without a shepherd" (Matt. 9:36). Such compassion should mark us and motivate our evangelism.

Compassionate love marked the evangelism of Paul. We read in Romans these words: "Brothers, my heart's desire and prayer to God for the Israelites is that they may be saved" (Rom. 10:1; cf. 9:1–5). Paul loved the lost, and so he shared the gospel with them. He wrote, "I am talking to you Gentiles. Inasmuch as I am the apostle to the Gentiles, I make much of my ministry in the hope that I may somehow arouse my own people to envy and save some of them" (Rom. 11:13–14). Paul loved them and, therefore, wanted to see them saved. So he was motivated, he told the Corinthians, to become "weak" if he needed to, in order to "save some" (1 Cor. 9:22).

Augustine talked about this over 1500 years ago. Speaking of Jesus' great command, he wrote:

> "Thou shalt love thy neighbor as thyself." Now you love yourself suitably when you love God better than yourself. What, then, you aim at in yourself you must aim at in your neighbor, namely, that he may love God with a perfect affection. For you do not love him as yourself, unless you try to draw him to that good which you are yourself pursuing. For this is the one good which has room for all to pursue it along with thee. From this precept proceed the duties of human society.[2]

The gospel helps us to love the lost. We are instructed by

God's own love. We are moved by the needs of the lost. We are compelled by Christ's sacrifice. And we feel, ourselves, the benefit of betraying our sins and turning to Christ in full trust. As we so experience the gospel, we find ourselves loving others more, and we want to share this good news with them.

Sometimes at our meetings of church elders or staff, we'll have to decide who gets to tell someone a piece of good news. Maybe it's a seminarian we've decided to support or a missionary. Maybe it's someone we want to ask to preach, or someone we've decided to approach about serving the church in a certain position, or a prospective intern whose application has been accepted. It's good news, and we know the recipients will like it, so we all want to be the one to tell them.

Can you imagine being less excited about telling someone the infinitely better news of the gospel of Jesus Christ? And, yet, too often we are. I am!

Evangelism is a duty of the Christian, and it is a duty born of love for others. And it's a privilege.

Love for God

Finally, though, our love for people can prove inadequate. The motivating force of our whole life, including our evangelism, must be our love for God.

> Love for God is the only sufficient motive for evangelism. Self-love will give way to self-centeredness; love for the lost will fail with those whom we cannot love, and when difficulties seem unsurmountable [sic], only a deep love for God will keep us following his way, declaring his Gospel, when human resources fail. Only our love for God—and, more important, his love for us—will keep us from the dangers which beset us. When the desire for popularity with men, or for success in human terms, tempts us to water down the

Gospel, to make it palatable, then only if we love God will we stand fast by his truth and his ways.[3]

Ultimately, our motive in evangelism must be a desire to see God glorified. This was the end of all of the Lord Jesus' actions (see John 17). Again and again throughout Ezekiel we read the phrase "then they will know that I am the LORD" as God's explanation for his actions with his disobedient people (e.g., Ezek. 12:16; 20:20; cf. verses about intra-Trinitarian love: John 3:35; 5:20; 14:31). Jesus taught that the actions of those who follow him would bring glory to his Father: "This is to my Father's glory, that you bear much fruit, showing yourselves to be my disciples" (John 15:8). So we share the gospel to glorify God, which happens as we declare the truth about God to his creation.

God is glorified in being known. To see others truly come to know him glorifies God and honors him. To tell the truth about one another does not necessarily convey honor. We have all done things that bring us shame rather than glory. But God is perfect. To tell the truth about God is to praise him, to glorify him. When others come to know him, it tells the truth about his *desirability*. This is why Christians like John Harper, whom I mentioned in the introduction, are so zealous to share the truth, the good news, about Jesus Christ.

The call to evangelism is a call to turn our lives outward from focusing on ourselves and our needs to focusing on God and on others made in his image who are still at enmity with him, alienated from him, and in need of salvation from sin and guilt. We bring God glory as we speak the truth about him to his creation. This is not the only way that we can bring glory to God, but it is one of the chief ways that he has given us as Christians, as those who know him through his grace in Christ. It is not a way that we will bring him glory eternally in heaven; it is one of the special privileges of living now, in this fallen world.

Peter exhorted Christians in the first century toward the glory of God: "Live such good lives among the pagans that, though they accuse you of doing wrong, they may see your good deeds and glorify God on the day he visits us" (1 Pet. 2:12). Peter knew that the Christian life that bears witness to God and the gospel will be a ground for God to be glorified in the last day. This is a never-ending motive to evangelize.

Sometimes we ignore even the most important things in our lives. There have been times when I've run out of gas while driving my car. I actually remember doing it twice in one summer! Just as with my disregard for a low gas tank, evangelism is one of those most important things that we can forget or ignore or neglect. We should commit ourselves to combat this neglect. So in order to help you do that, let me finish off this chapter with some encouragements to evangelize.

Encouragements to Evangelize

Following are five simple practices to encourage you in evangelism.

1) **Ask for testimonies.** As I mentioned in chapter 5, I love hearing people share how they came to Christ. I am encouraged to share the gospel with others as I hear such stories. I am reminded of the change Christ has made in my own life and in the lives of so many others I know and love.

In order to join our church, you must meet with me (or with one of the other elders), and part of what we ask you to do is to share your testimony with us. That is one of my favorite parts of being a pastor. I've gotten to sit and listen to literally hundreds of people share how they've come to Christ. And they've come in all kinds of ways, but it's always Christ they've come to by repenting of their sins and trusting in him.

And, inevitably, how did they get to that point? They came to Christ because someone shared the gospel with them.

2) Consider the reality of hell. I do think about the shortness of this life, and I think about the life to come. I think about people meeting God in his wrath. As one Puritan said, "Outside of Christ, God is terrible." Do you understand what he meant? He meant that God is good, and because he is unswervingly, uncompromisingly, unerringly good, he will not accept any kind of evil. As the prophet Habakkuk said to God, "Your eyes are too pure to look on evil; you cannot tolerate wrong" (Hab. 1:13).

Since that's the case, it's no surprise that God is committed to punish those who are in rebellion against him, those who are in sins that they will not repent of. And the penalty is not merely an annihilation or an absence but the active punishment of the sinner for their sins. And that state of being punished forever for those sins you will not repent of is called hell.

Thinking of such things sobers me. It clarifies what the big issues are in my day and my week. Remembering this truth helps me in conversations with people that I meet. Not that I immediately or always think, "This person is going to hell." But I do think, "This is a person who is liable to fall under God's wrath. I want to share with them the wonderful work that Christ has performed for all who will turn from their sins and trust in him!"

Apart from such turning and trusting, however, there is only God's deserved wrath. We read in John 3:36: "Whoever believes in the Son has eternal life, but whoever rejects the Son will not see life, for God's wrath remains on him." How will someone ever escape this wrath? They never will, unless they come to believe in the Son. But how will they come to believe? It will happen only by someone sharing the gospel with them.

3) **Consider God's sovereignty.** This one may surprise you, but I'm actually just following God's lead in pointing out the doctrine of his sovereignty. Paul was becoming a reluctant evangelist—or at least a tired and discouraged one—in Corinth. We read in Acts 18:9–11: "One night the Lord spoke to Paul in a vision: 'Do not be afraid; keep on speaking, do not be silent. For I am with you, and no one is going to attack and harm you, because I have many people in this city.'" When the Lord said that he "had many people in this city," he wasn't referring to Corinth's population; Paul was surely aware already of the size of the city. So then what was the Lord saying to Paul?

God was telling Paul that the fact that God had elected some (in this case, many, in Corinth) for salvation meant that Paul should continue preaching so that the elect would be saved. Paul knew that God had willed Paul's evangelism to bear such good fruit.

Have you heard it said that the doctrine of God's choosing some for salvation (the doctrine of election) undercuts evangelism? It didn't in Paul's life. As he later wrote to Timothy, "I endure everything for the sake of the elect, that they too may obtain the salvation that is in Christ Jesus, with eternal glory" (2 Tim. 2:10). Romans 10 contains Paul's clearest and most impassioned plea for Christians to send out people to preach the gospel because it is the only way people are saved; but this impassioned plea comes after what many consider Paul's plainest teaching about the doctrine of election in Romans 9. He didn't see any inconsistency that a sovereign God is also a saving God.

Somehow, Paul found the doctrine of God's sovereignty an encouragement in his evangelism. Do we need to recover this confidence in a day of increasing opposition to the public preaching of the gospel? I think that we do. I fear that much of today's evangelism will soon end. As evangelism becomes more and more unpopular, I fear that some Christians will simply dilute it, water it down, alter it, or even stop sharing the good news altogether. I think a better understanding of the Bible's teaching on God's election would help them. I think it would give them confidence and joy in their evangelism.

But isn't the doctrine of election not only narrow-minded but also narrow-hearted? I know some people think so. I like the prayer I've heard attributed to C. H. Spurgeon: "Lord, save the elect, and elect some more." I don't mean that disrespectfully. I'm sure I could never be more generous than God. But I'm also sure that God is not disappointed by our aspirations that more and more people should come to know him in his wonderful, majestic, saving love. But how will they come to know God's love? They will only do so by someone sharing the gospel with them.

4) **Meditate on the gospel.** I find the gospel message itself compelling. To think about who God is (for the Christian) is to be attracted to him. It is to be enthused. It is to be drawn to him and his heart, to his holiness and his just claims on our allegiance.

Meditating on man's need is also an encouragement to evangelize. Man's need concerns more than just his eternal state; it also involves his current enslavement by and to sin. Such a creature, made in the image of God, should not be spending his life in rebellion, as if there were a better government for his soul than God's. He should, rather, be in fellowship with God, submitted to him, and adopted as God's own child. How can someone so repent of their sins and believe in Christ? It is only by someone sharing the gospel with him.

5) **Consider the cross.** Meditating, too, on what God has provided in Christ is a special encouragement to share the gospel. To think that God has loved us at all is amazing, con-

sidering how we have treated him. But to think of him loving us to the extent that he has in Christ—this is *truly* amazing. He bought the church with his blood (Acts 20:28). On the cross, Christ showed us the extent of God's love; would you know its height and breadth and depth and length? Then look at Christ's arms outstretched on the cross.

Perhaps you have sometime in your life received a gift that absolutely embarrassed you. The expense of the gift, its rarity, or even the sheer thoughtfulness so overwhelmed you that you almost wanted to shrink back from it. That's the way it is with the cross of Christ. We almost can't believe that Someone so good could love people like us, and love us so thoroughly and to that extent!

How can someone come to know the beauty of God's love in the cross of Christ? Only by someone sharing the gospel with them. In light of all this, evangelism should be both a discipline and a worshipful act of devotion.

I thought that this was going to be a small book on evangelism, but it's getting to be a big one! I'd better bring this thing to a conclusion. Before you go, I want us to think together about "closing the sale."

Conclusion
Closing the Sale

So this is the end. Almost.

This is to be our evangelism: a God-given commission and method, a God-centered message, and a God-centered motive. We should all evangelize. Evangelism isn't all those other things we considered; it is telling the good news about Jesus, and doing it with honesty, urgency, and joy, using the Bible, living a life that backs it up, and praying, and doing it all for the glory of God.

I remember reading a little book by C. S. Lovett, *Soul-winning Made Easy*, in which Lovett lays out a "Soul-Winning Plan," as he calls it, which is based on sales techniques of the time. "You are in command," he says, talking about Christians as salesmen.

In much the same way the trained soul-winner can bring his prospect to a decision for Christ. There is no middle ground as he moves with surety and deftness right up to the point of salvation. It is his conversation control that makes this possible. He knows exactly what he is going to say each step of the way and can even anticipate his prospect's responses. He is able to keep the conversation focused on the main issue and prevent unrelated materials from being introduced. The controlled conversation technique is something new in evangelism and represents a real break-through in soul-winning.[1]

Lovett then instructs the earnest Christian about various tools needed and gives some helpful hints such as, "Get your prospect alone."[2] At one point, he teaches how to press for the decision. He writes, "Lay your hand firmly on the subject's shoulder (or arm) with a semi-commanding tone of voice, and say to him: 'Bow your head with me.' Note: Do not look at him when you say this, but bow your head first. Out of the corner of your eye you will see him hesitate at first. Then, as his resistance crumbles, his head will come down. Your hand on his shoulder will feel the relaxation and you will know when his heart yields. Bowing your head first causes terrific psychological pressure."[3] It causes terrific psychological pressure.

Terrific psychological pressure. Psychological pressure. Pressure. How many churches today are full of people who have been psychologically pressured but never truly converted?

At my church in Washington, we had a visitor one Sunday who came up to me at the door after the service. He had appreciated the message and wanted to tell me so. I steeled myself for the encouragement. After he told me that the sermon was good in various ways, he characterized it as "perhaps the best sales pitch I have ever heard. And," he added, "that should mean something, because that's what I do for a living. I'm a salesman."

At this point I was trying to accept the remark kindly, feigning slight but godly humility, all the time beginning to chew on the compliment like a dog on a bone.

"But" he added, "I have one criticism."

"What's that?" I asked, honestly curious.

"You didn't close the sale!" And with that statement, it was like an adult had just entered a room of childish daydreams. My attention snapped to. I saw a different view on the gospel and evangelism, one that pivoted on that one statement.

We need to know what kind of sales we can close and what

kind we can't. The redemption of an eternal soul is one sale that we, in our own strength, cannot accomplish. And we need to know it, not so that we won't preach the gospel, but so that we won't allow the gospel that is preached to be molded by what finally gets a response!

That last sentence was important, so I'm going to repeat it. We need to know what "sales" we can "close" and what "sales" we *can't*—not so that we won't preach the gospel, but so that we won't allow the gospel that is preached to be molded by what finally gets a response.

As I was falling asleep last night, I read an essay by the late liberal theologian Paul Tillich.[4] In this essay, Tillich suggested that Christianity has powerful symbols (creation, fall, incarnation, salvation, heaven), which lose their connection with modern life when they are taken literally. My salesman friend sounded like a modern disciple of Tillich. You can close the sale. If you don't get a response, change the way you present the message until you do get a response—until you can close the sale. That can get perilously close to changing the message.[5]

You and I aren't called to use our extensive powers to convict and change the sinner while God stands back as a gentleman, quietly waiting for the spiritual corpse, his declared spiritual enemy, to invite God into his heart. Rather, we should resolve to preach the gospel like gentlemen, persuading while knowing we can't regenerate anyone, and then stand back while God uses all his extensive powers to convict and change the sinner. Then we'll see clearly who it is that can really call the dead to life, and although he'll use us in the doing of it, it's not you and I who are actually doing it.

God can use anybody, and he likes to do just that for his own glory. He used Moses the stutterer to confront the world's mightiest king and to bring God's law to his people. God used Paul the Jewish nationalist to reach the Gentiles.

George Whitefield, the great eighteenth-century evangelist, was hounded by a group of detractors who called themselves the Hell-fire Club. They derided his work and mocked him. On one occasion, one of them, a man named Thorpe, preached a sermon in which he mimicked Whitefield to his cronies with brilliant accuracy, perfectly imitating Whitefield's tone and facial expressions. When Thorpe himself was so pierced that he sat down and was converted on the spot.[6]

The gospel is powerful, and God is committed to using this good news through our spreading of it to every tribe and tongue and people and nation on earth.

Sometimes the charge is leveled, "If you're a believer in election, you won't evangelize." But haven't many of the greatest evangelists in the history of the Christian church believed that salvation is by God's election? Has that dulled the evangelistic zeal of a Whitefield or an Edwards, of a Carey or a Judson, of a Spurgeon or a Lloyd-Jones, of a D. James Kennedy or an R. C. Sproul.

My concern is the opposite: if you *don't* believe that the gospel is the good news of God's action—the Father electing, the Son dying, the Spirit drawing—that conversion is only our response to God's giving us the grace-gifts of repentance and faith, and that evangelism is our simple, faithful, prayerful telling of this good news, then you will actually damage the evangelistic mission of the church by making false converts. If you think that the gospel is all about what we can do, that the practice of it is optional, and that conversion is simply something that anyone can choose at any time, then I'm concerned that you'll think of evangelism as nothing more than a sales job where the prospect is to be won over to sign on the dotted line by praying a prayer, followed by an assurance that he is the proud owner of salvation.

But evangelism isn't all about our ability to hawk our

religious wares. Discouragement can be painfully sharp sometimes as we share this best of news only to have it received as unimportant or unbelievable. But that's where we must remember that it is our part simply to give out the message; God will bring the increase.

I pray that we see an end to a wrong, shallow view of evangelism that simply tries to get people to say yes to a question or to make a one-time decision. As David Wells recently said, "We live in a day when it is very easy to make converts, very hard to make disciples." Of course, such non-disciple converts are no true converts, so we want to see an end to the bad fruit of false evangelism:

- worldly people feeling assurance because they made a decision one time;
- real revival being lost amid our own manufactured and scheduled meetings that we euphemistically call "revivals" (as if we could determine where and when the wind of God's Spirit will move);
- church memberships markedly larger than the number of those involved with the church;
- inaction in our own lives, as we ignore the evangelistic mandate—the call to share the good news. We want to see the end of this debilitating, deadly coldness to the glorious call to tell the good news.

We want to see a renewed commitment to and joy in the great privilege we have of sharing the good news of Christ with the lost and dying world around us. Only because Someone Else was so faithful can anyone be saved.

Pray that God will use you as a faithful messenger of the good news. Pray that you will see others saved from God's good punishment for their sins because they accept the good news of Christ's substitutionary death. And if God, in his mysterious sovereignty, ordains it not to be so with those to whom we witness, may it not be because we have failed in our commission to make him and his grace in Christ known to every creature made in his image. This good news of Jesus Christ is crucial. Until you recognize that, I can say nothing helpful to you about evangelism. It will be no more for you than an unpleasant duty or an occasional impulse. When the message of the cross captures your heart, then your tongue—stammering, halting, insulting, awkward, sarcastic, and imperfect as it may be—won't be far behind. As Jesus said, "Out of the overflow of the heart the mouth speaks" (Matt. 12:34).

What is your heart full of?

What do you spend your words on?

The Christian call to evangelism is not simply a call to persuade people to make decisions, but rather to proclaim to them the good news of salvation in Christ, to call them to repentance, and to give God the glory for regeneration and conversion.

We do not fail in our evangelism if we faithfully tell the gospel to someone who is not subsequently converted; we fail only if we do not faithfully tell the gospel at all.

Recommended Reading

A few suggestions for further reading in evangelism are these:

- Will Metzger's *Tell the Truth*, rev. ed. (InterVarsity Press, 2002) may be the single best book on evangelism that I've read. Metzger makes it clear both theologically and practically that our evangelism should not be "man-centered" but "God-centered." The book contains old illustrations and good charts.
- Mack Stiles's *Speaking of Jesus* (InterVarsity Press, 1995) provides masterful examples of naturally speaking about Jesus Christ to friends and family. Mack is one of the best personal evangelists I have ever met and never ceases to exhibit a personal and spiritual empathy for those around him. His ability to relate and remember spills over into his book in the entertaining and instructive stories he recounts.
- Iain Murray's *Revival and Revivalism* (Banner of Truth, 1994) recounts some crucial changes in the history and practice of evangelism that still affect us negatively today.
- J. I. Packer's *Evangelism & the Sovereignty of God* (InterVarsity Press, 1991) is a modern classic in explaining the theology of Christian activity in evangelism and how that fits with the Bible's teaching on God's election. This is a great introduction to a doctrine (election) that God used to encourage Paul in his evangelism (see Acts 18).
- Among resources pertaining specifically to the actual gospel, I know of nothing better (outside of the Bible) to sug-

gest to you than the canons of the synod of Dort. Look them up, then read them and meditate on them slowly, carefully, paragraph by paragraph. Be amazed at God's love for us in Christ. Also, Robert Letham's book *The Work of Christ* (InterVarsity, 1993) is a great meditation on the center of the gospel.

- Tools to consider using for doing evangelism are *Christianity Explained* (Scripture Union) and *Two Ways to Live* (Matthias Media).
- More tools and articles on evangelism can be found at www.9marks.org.

Appendix
A Word to Pastors

Many people feel that evangelism should be left up to pastors. (We thought about that back in chapter 3.) The truth is that pastors often have an especially hard time finding ways to do personal evangelism.

Think about it. We pastors spend our workdays with Christians. We spend our evenings with our families, or church officers, and maybe the occasional neighbor or other friend. How can we pastors evangelize? We need to for all the reasons other Christians need to and also to serve as models.

First, we must remember that our preaching is the primary way that God has uniquely called us to evangelize.[1] We want to preach the gospel to non-Christians, and we desire to see the fruit of conversions.

To this end, we should be careful to include a summary of the gospel in every sermon. I remember my friend Bill coming up to me after I had preached a sermon on Lamentations. He told me that it was a good sermon, and then, after a pause, he asked me something like, "But did you have the gospel in the sermon?"

I was surprised by the question, but as I later went back and examined the sermon, I found that I had nowhere clearly explained what Christ had done, and how he calls us to repent and believe. I resolved from that point on to try always to clearly present the gospel in each sermon.

Other truths, too, in our sermons can help in our evangelism, and we can help Christians listening to us preach by modeling how to speak the truth. Plough up the ground often by speaking of God's holiness and our sin. Be clear about the problem of our sin in relation to a God who is all good. Try to expose Satan's lie that sin is petty. Try to help people see sin's weightiness and the depth of its opposition to God.

Make sure that your sermons both instruct people about the gospel and appeal to people to respond to it. If you make an appeal without the instruction, you are making an assumption that your listeners understand the gospel, when they may not really know what it is. On the other hand, if you only tell gospel truths in the third person, in other words, if you tell only your experience of it, then people may not understand that the Bible teaches clearly that they themselves are to repent and believe.

Be available after preaching also. Stand at the door, go to the reception, somehow make yourself available to folks who have just heard you deliver God's Word, and who, therefore, may have special questions about how the message relates to them or about particular issues that they want to understand more fully.

My pastor friend, even beyond your preaching, be sure to pray regularly for non-Christian neighbors, friends, and family. Pray publicly for conversions in your pastoral prayers before the sermon. Encourage and model praying for God to save non-Christians. And spend time thanking God for your own salvation; keep your gratitude fresh.

Pray to be a faithful evangelist as well. I have in the past gone regularly to certain restaurants, shopped at certain stores, and frequented certain places of business in order to build relationships in those places as opportunities for sharing the gospel. Undertaking personal evangelism of this nature requires being a patient customer, a good tipper, and a conversationalist—even when you may not have budgeted the time for it. Realize, too, that you are called to equip the saints to evangelize. C. H. Spurgeon said:

> With all that you can do your desires will not be fulfilled, for soul-winning is a pursuit which grows upon a man; the more he is rewarded with Conversions the more eager he becomes to see greater numbers born unto God. Hence you will soon discover that *you need help if many are to be brought in*. The net soon becomes too heavy for one pair of hands to drag to shore when it is filled with fishes; and your fellow-helpers must be beckoned to your assistance. Great things are done by the Holy Spirit when a whole church is aroused to sacred energy. . . . Contemplate at the outset the possibility of having a church of soul-winners. Do not succumb to the usual idea that we can only gather a few useful workers, and that the rest of the community must inevitably be a dead weight: it may possibly so happen, but do not set out with that notion or it will be verified. The usual need not be the universal; better things are possible than anything yet attained; set your aim high and spare no effort to reach it. Labor to gather a church alive for Jesus, every member energetic to the full, and the whole in incessant activity for the salvation of men. To this end there must be the best of preaching to feed the host into strength, continual prayer to bring down the power from on high, and the most heroic example on your own part to fire their zeal.

The pastor should make sure that others in the congregation are equipped in evangelism. We can equip not only through our preaching, but by our conversations, the books we give out, the way we admit new members (we always ask them to recount the gospel and their testimony with us). We can provide the congregation with training in specific evangelistic tools (such as *Christianity Explained* or *Two Ways to Live*[2]). We can model a concern for evangelism and conversions in our prayers. We can sponsor special evangelistic events. We can encourage the members by having times for sharing and praying in which we specifically pray for evangelistic initiatives and for particular conversions.

Through all this, we must lead by example. As pastors, we are called to lead by our teaching but also by our actions. So we must heed Paul's charge to Timothy: "But you, keep your head in all situations, endure hardship, do the work of an evangelist, discharge all the duties of your ministry" (2 Tim. 4:5). In everything, from our personal prayer life to conversations with family and neighbors, we should work to present Christ well.

We pastors should accept the role of leadership that God has given us. Certainly, we pastors sacrifice personal opportunities to do evangelism when we work full-time in ministry. We are, in a sense, willing to be pulled behind the front lines in order to equip others. We realize the front line of the contest, the "skin" of the church, if you will, is represented by the members of the local congregation after they leave church on Sunday. It is then, throughout the week, that the church presses in on the kingdom of darkness as believers live out their callings around hundreds or even thousands of non-Christians each week. It is our task as pastors to lead all believers in accepting, embracing, and using the opportunities that God richly gives them. In all of this, we should work not so much merely to implement programs as to create a culture in our church. We want our congregations to be marked by a culture of evangelism. In order to do that, we are going to have to watch how many nights we encourage our members to be doing some program at church. We must give our members time to develop friendships with non-Christians.

So, my pastor friend, be encouraged in evangelism. Share stories about evangelism with your friends. Ask them to recount recent evangelistic experiences. Read books that remind you of the priority of evangelism in your own ministry. Let me suggest a few that kindle my own soul: Richard Baxter, *The Reformed Pastor*; Charles Bridges, *The Christian Ministry*; Horatius Bonar, *Words to the Winners of Souls*; C. H. Spurgeon, *Lectures to My Students* (or, really, anything by Spurgeon).

Notes

Introduction

1. Moody Adams, *The Titanic's Last Hero: Story About John Harper* (Columbia, SC: Olive Press, 1997), 24–25.

Chapter One

1. Everett Gill, *A Biography of A. T. Robertson* (New York: Macmillan, 1943), 187.

Chapter Two

1. Thomas A. Harris, *I'm Okay, You're Okay: A Practical Guide to Transitional Analysis* (New York: Avon, 1969).

2. John Calvin, *Institutes of the Christian Religion*, 2 Vols., in The Library of Christian Classics, Vol. 20, ed. John T. McNeil (Philadelphia: Westminster Press, 1960), 1.1.35.

3. J. C. Ryle, *Holiness* (1883; repr., Grand Rapids, MI: Baker, 1979), 204.

Chapter Three

1. For more on this question, see Robert Plummer, "Paul's Understanding of the Church's Mission: Did the Apostle Paul Expect the Early Christian Communities to Evangelize?" (Carlisle, UK: Paternoster Biblical Monographs, 2006).

2. John Stott, *Personal Evangelism* (Downers Grove, IL: InterVarsity; 1949), 3–4.

3. This is Rob Plummer's conclusion in his excellent study cited above. "The apostolic mission devolves upon each church as a whole—not upon any particular member or group. Each individual member within the church, then, will manifest missionary

activity according to his or her particular gifting and life situation. All but the unrepeatable aspects of the apostles' mission
(e.g., eyewitness testimony and initial promulgation of authorita-
tive revelation) devolve upon the church as a whole." Plummer,
"Paul's Understanding of the Church's Mission," 144.

4. John Stott, "Why Don't They Listen?" *Christianity Today* (September 2003): 52.

5. Iain H. Murray, *D. Martyn Lloyd-Jones: The First Forty Years
1899–1939* (Edinburgh: Banner of Truth, 1983), 246.

6. John Bunyan, *Grace Abounding to the Chief of Sinners* (1875;
repr., Grand Rapids, MI: Baker, 1986), 29–30, 37–40.

7. Donna Britt, "Love Stories That Transcend Bonds of Slavery,
Time," *Washington Post* (February 11, 2005), in Betty DeRamus,
Forbidden Fruit: Love Stories from the Underground Railroad
(New York: Atria, 2005), 15–27.

Chapter Four

1. Robert Schuller, *Milk & Honey* (December 1997): 4.

2. For more on this topic, see J. I. Packer, *Evangelism and the Sovereignty of God* (Downers Grove, IL: InterVarsity, 1991).

3. Two books that have excellent examples of conversations are
Mack Stiles, *Speaking of Jesus* (Downers Grove, IL: InterVarsity,
1995), and Randy Newman, *Corner Conversations* (Grand Rapids, MI: Kregel, 2006).

Chapter Five

1. Graham Johnston, *Preaching to a Postmodern World* (Grand
Rapids, MI: Baker, 2001), 136.

2. Donald McGavran, "The Dimensions of World Evangelization,"
in *Let the Earth Hear His Voice,* ed. J. D. Douglas (Worldwide
Publications, 1975), 109.

3. John Stott, "The Biblical Basis of Evangelism," in *Let the Earth
Hear His Voice,* ed. J. D. Douglas, 69.

4. "The Lausanne Covenant," in *Let the Earth Hear His Voice,* ed.
J. D. Douglas, 4.

5. John Cheeseman, *Saving Grace* (Edinburgh: Banner of Truth,
1999), 113.

6. D. Martyn Lloyd-Jones, *Preaching & Preachers* (Grand Rapids,
MI: Zondervan, 1971), 276.

7. Cecil Sherman, "Hard Times Make for Hard Thinking," in *Why
I Am a Baptist: Reflections on Being Baptist in the 21st Cen-*

tury, ed. Cecil P. Staton (Macon, GA: Smyth & Helwys, 1999), 136–37.

8. John Flavel, *Mystery of Providence* (1678; repr., Edinburgh: Banner of Truth, 1963), 11.

Chapter Six

1. In Mark 9:40 Jesus says, "Whoever is not against us if for us" (see also Luke 9:50). Here, however, he seems to be speaking to the disciples regarding good work done in Christ's name by someone who wasn't one of their number. In the statements in Mark 12:30 and Luke 11:23, Jesus seems to be warning unbelieving religious leaders about the danger of indifference to him.

2. A great evangelistic presentation that majors on this dichotomy is *Two Ways to Live* (Kingsford, Australia: Matthias Media, 1989). Or see an online presentation at http://www.matthiasmedia.com. au/2wtl/.

3. D. Martyn Lloyd-Jones, *Preaching & Preachers* (Grand Rapids, MI: Zondervan, 1972), 276.

4. Carey Hardy, "Just as I Am," in *Fool's Gold,* ed. John MacArthur (Wheaton, IL: Crossway, 2005), 136–37.

Chapter Seven

1. Robert Jenson, "The God-Wars," in *Either/Or: The Gospel or Neopaganism,* ed. Carl E. Braaten and Robert W. Jenson (Grand Rapids, MI: Eerdmans, 1995), 25.

2. Augustine, "Morals of the Catholic Church," in *The Nicene and Post-Nicene Fathers,* Vol. 4, ed. Philip Schaff (Peabody, MA: Hendrickson, 1994), 55.

3. John Cheeseman et al., *The Grace of God in the Gospel* (Edinburgh: Banner of Truth, 1972), 122. For some reason, this paragraph was not retained in John Cheeseman's revision of this book, *Saving Grace* (Edinburgh: Banner of Truth, 1999).

Conclusion

1. C. S. Lovett, *Soul-winning Made Easy* (Lockman Foundation, 1959), 17–18.

2. Lovett, *Soul-winning Made Easy,* 23.

3. Lovett, *Soul-winning Made Easy,* 50.

4. Paul Tillich, "The Lost Dimension in Religion," in *Adventures of the Mind,* ed. Richard Thruelson and John Kobler (New York: Vintage, 1958) 52–62.

5. A concern for evangelistic outreach has often been the path to liberalism. This is in no way to suggest that a concern for evangelism is bad—it's essential!—It's just more dangerous than is often recognized. For more on this, see the writings of Iain Murray, especially *Revival and Revivalism* (Edinburgh: Banner of Truth, 1994), and *Evangelicalism Divided: A Record of Crucial Change in the Years 1950–2000* (Edinburgh: Banner of Truth, 2000).

6. Spurgeon recounts this in *Metropolitan Tabernacle Pulpit,* 34: 115.

Appendix

1. See my chapter, "Evangelistic Expository Preaching," in Philip Graham Ryken et al., *Give Praise to God* (Phillipsburg, NJ: P&R 2003), 122–39.

2. *Two Ways to Live* (Kingsford NSW, Australia: Matthias Media, 2003); *Christianity Explained* (Valley Forge, PA: Scripture Union, 1975).

9Marks

Building Healthy Churches

9Marks exists to equip church leaders with a biblical vision and practical resources for displaying God's glory to the nations through healthy churches.

To that end, we want to see churches characterized by these nine marks of health:

1   Expositional Preaching
2   Biblical Theology
3   A Biblical Understanding of the Gospel
4   A Biblical Understanding of Conversion
5   A Biblical Understanding of Evangelism
6   Biblical Church Membership
7   Biblical Church Discipline
8   Biblical Discipleship
9   Biblical Church Leadership

Find all our Crossway titles
and other resources at
www.9Marks.org